In My Opinion . . .

We're working to make the best possible materials available for continuing education and we want to know how we're doing. After you've completed your continuing education course, please take a few moments to answer the following questions and mail the form back to us. Thanks for your help!

1. What is the title of the continuing education book you are using?

2. Did you use this booklet in a:

   ☐ classroom course   ☐ home study/correspondence course

3. What license do you hold:

   ☐ salesperson   ☐ broker   ☐ other_____

4. Please rate the booklet on the following:

	Excellent	Good	Fair	Poor
overall content	☐	☐	☐	☐
accuracy	☐	☐	☐	☐
organization	☐	☐	☐	☐
other				

5. What features or topics did you like the best?

6. How can we make this booklet a better continuing education tool?

7. What other topics would you like to cover in your continuing education courses?

IMPORTANT—PLEASE FOLD OVER—PLEASE TAPE BEFORE MAILING

> **NOTE:** This page, when folded over and taped, becomes an envelope, which has been approved by the United States Postal Service. It is provided for your convenience.

IMPORTANT—PLEASE FOLD OVER—PLEASE TAPE BEFORE MAILING

Return Address:

BUSINESS REPLY MAIL
FIRST CLASS MAIL   PERMIT NO. 88176   CHICAGO, IL

POSTAGE WILL BE PAID BY ADDRESSEE:

Real Estate Education Company

a division of Dearborn Financial Publishing, Inc.

Attn. Diana Faulhaber
155 N. Wacker Drive
Chicago, IL 60606-9548

No Postage Necessary if Mailed in the United States

IMPORTANT—PLEASE FOLD OVER—PLEASE TAPE BEFORE MAILING

> **NOTE:** This page, when folded over and taped, becomes an envelope, which has been approved by the United States Postal Service. It is provided for your convenience.

IMPORTANT—PLEASE FOLD OVER—PLEASE TAPE BEFORE MAILING

JAMES C. PRENDERGAST

red flags
property inspection guide

Real Estate Education Company
a division of Dearborn Financial Publishing, Inc.

While a great deal of care has been taken to provide accurate and current information, the ideas, suggestions, general principles and conclusions presented in this book are subject to local, state and federal laws and regulations, court cases and any revisions of same. The reader is thus urged to consult legal counsel regarding any points of law—this publication should not be used as a substitute for competent legal advice.

Publisher: Carol L. Luitjens
Acquisitions Editor: Diana Faulhaber
Project Editor: Debra M. Hall
Art Manager: Lucy Jenkins
Cover Designer: Daniel Christmas, Design Alliance, Inc.

© 1995 by Dearborn Financial Publishing, Inc.®

Published by Real Estate Education Company,
a division of Dearborn Financial Publishing, Inc.®

All rights reserved. The text of this publication, or any part thereof, may not be reproduced in any manner whatsoever without permission in writing from the publisher.

Printed in the United States of America.

95 96 97 10 9 8 7 6 5 4 3 2 1

Library of Congress Cataloging-in-Publication Data

Prendergast, James C.
    Red flags / James C. Prendergast.
       p.   cm.
    ISBN 0-7931-1203-6
    1. Dwellings—Inspection.   I. Title.
    TH4817.5.P74   1994
    643'.12—dc20
                            94-24326
                               CIP

TABLE OF CONTENTS

PREFACE

LESSON ONE RED FLAGS--WHAT ARE THEY AND WHAT CAUSES THEM? 1

    Learning Objectives
    What Are Distressed Structures, and What
        Should Homeowners and Brokers Do
        About Them?
    What Is a Red Flag?
    Research and Planning
    What Are the Causes For Damage In
        Structures?
    Expansive Soils
    Fills
    Freezing Ground
    Collapsing Soils, Sinkholes, Voids
    Landsliding
    Poor Drainage
    Structural Defects
    Lesson One Quiz

LESSON TWO INSPECTING FOR RED FLAGS OUTSIDE THE HOME 10

    Learning Objectives
    Cracks in Sidewalks, Driveways and Decks
    Cracks in Foundations
    Visually Distorted Structure
    Drainage
    Building Ventilation
    Hillside Instability, Landsliding
    Fills
    Roof, Window, and Flashing Leakage
    Hazardous Vegetation
    Hazardous Railings
    Hazardous Stairs
    Hazardous Walkways and Steps
    Septic Systems
    Garage Door Springs
    Retaining Walls
    Swimming Pools and Spas
    Tennis Courts
    Play Structures
    Illegal Additions
    Lesson Two Quiz

LESSON THREE   **INSPECTING FOR RED FLAGS INSIDE THE HOME**   29

        Learning Objectives
        Basements and Crawl Spaces
        Wall Cracks
        Concealed Red Flags
        House Alignment
        Fireplaces
        Sagging Beams
        Major Mechanical Systems
        Stairways
        Glass
        Smoke Alarms
        Other Safety Hazards
        Lesson Three Quiz

LESSON FOUR   **RED FLAGS ASSOCIATED WITH ENVIRONMENTAL**   44
        HAZARDS AND HAZARDOUS MATERIALS

        Learning Objectives
        Hazardous Materials
        Asbestos
        Stoves and Furnaces
        Walls and Pipes
        Appliances
        Roofing Shingles, and Siding
        How to Identify Asbestos
        Toxic Waste
        Radon
        Underground Storage Tanks/Hazardous Waste
        Lead Hazards From Pipes and Paint
        Lesson Four Quiz

PREFACE

In medicine, pain is a symptom of illness or injury. In a home, sloping floors, cracked walls and foundations are visible symptoms of structural distress that point to possible defects or safety hazards; such symptoms are called Red Flags.

A home is usually the most important purchase in anyone's life, and new homeowners who discover significant problems after they have moved in are rightfully indignant. Often, problems cost many thousands of dollars to correct, or they adversely affect a home's resale value, or an unsafe condition may contribute to an injury. In such cases, a buyer often looks for someone to blame and files suit against the seller, usually including the real estate brokers involved in the purchase.

Real estate brokers and agents have always been responsible for faithfully representing the condition of a property without concealing any known defects. Recently, the courts and legislatures of various states, notably California, have given brokers and agents the additional duty of inspecting a property for any visible defects (Red Flags) that may affect its value or desirability, and of disclosing them to prospective buyers. This is a growing trend and real estate professionals nationwide will soon be required to inspect properties for Red Flags. **For the purposes of this course, a Red Flag is defined as a visual sign or indication of a defect.**

Some defects can be remedied by a few minutes work or a few dollars expended while others could lead to major property devaluation. Particular attention should be paid to Red Flags concerning the basic structural elements of the home such as foundations, floors, walls, and roofs.

Brokers and agents who understand their state's disclosure laws and learn to comply with them stand a much better chance of avoiding claims against themselves.

This course includes detailed home inspection techniques with illustrations and background information on asbestos, radon, lead, and other hazards to homeowners. It is hoped that it will be an effective tool for non-experts who need a guide to detect Red Flags in residential properties.

ABOUT THE AUTHOR

James C. Prendergast is a licensed civil engineer, geologist, and engineering geologist. He earned his B.S. in geology from the University of California, Riverside, and a M.S. in civil engineering--with a specialty in geotechnical engineering--at San Jose State University in California.

Mr. Prendergast has been active in the geotechnical field since 1968. In 1976 he founded the consulting firm JCP Geologists, Inc., in the San Francisco Bay Area. His firm has worked closely with real estate professionals, providing disclosure information on geologic hazard zones, as required by city, county and state laws, and the National Flood Insurance Program (NFIP).

In addition, the firm of JCP Geologists, Inc. provides a number of different products to the real estate profession in California including reports on geologic hazards, environmental hazards reports, "Red Flag" property inspections and home inspections.

LESSON ONE

RED FLAGS--WHAT ARE THEY AND WHAT CAUSES THEM?

LEARNING OBJECTIVES

Upon completion of Lesson One you will:

1. Understand the meaning of the term "Red Flag."

2. Learn why "Red Flags" are present in a home.

3. Be aware of the most common conditions that cause "Red Flags."

4. Know who to contact for advice in various "Red Flag" situations.

WHAT ARE DISTRESSED STRUCTURES, AND WHAT SHOULD HOMEOWNERS AND BROKERS DO ABOUT THEM?

A structure can be damaged or distressed in a short period of time, as in cases of floods, tornadoes, hurricanes, or earthquakes. More often, however, damage develops over many years and is caused by leaking roofs, settling fill or expanding soils, freezing or thawing ground, and slow moving landslides.

If a house's entire foundation moved evenly up or down one or two inches, like a houseboat rising and falling on a tide, damage--if any--would be minimal. However, the structure of a house is complex, and so is its interaction with the soil. When a foundation moves, it moves unevenly, one corner may settle an inch while the rest of the home remains stable.

Unstable foundations are a major cause of structural distress. The differential movement they cause creates pressure build-up, which concentrates at the corners of windows, doors, rooms, and at other places where structural members meet within walls. If the pressure is greater than the strength of the structure, weak, rigid parts will break and move.

Movement of portions of a building can also be caused by structural problems which could be related to the original design of the structure or to the quality of its construction. In general, observed Red Flags that indicate distress to a structure are very similar regardless of their underlying causes.

Lesson One

Coupled with poorly designed structural elements, poor drainage, and loose fill, "geologic processes" like landslides or freezing ground can shift a structure's foundation unevenly. These processes go through cycles of activity, and their effects build up over a period of years.

Patching cracks in walls, shaving doors, and re-leveling floors with jacks are only temporary fixes to any structural problem. Movement will continue until a repair scheme corrects the basic cause of the problem or designs around the problem. If a seller patches and paints a distressed house before selling it, without repairing the cause of the problem, the buyer of an apparently undamaged home that starts to crack and settle after title is transferred may have no alternative but to file suit against the seller and all parties involved in the transaction.

Since most serious distress is caused by foundation or soil problems, repair can be expensive, but it is in the interest of an owner or buyer of a distressed home to have it repaired properly to prevent further damage. In some cases, the only way to deliver a sound home to the buyer is to correct damage at the seller's expense.

An engineer with expertise in distressed structures should be consulted. The engineer will document the damage and determine the probable cause, do an in-depth study that often includes drilling for soil samples, and develop a repair scheme for which a contractor provides an estimate. Engineers can often recommend specialty contractors experienced in fixing such distressed homes.

Homeowners' insurance policies sometimes cover damaged structures. If an insurance company denies coverage, an attorney should be consulted. Contractors and developers may also be liable for improper construction. Again, experienced engineers usually know attorneys who are expert in this type of litigation.

WHAT IS A RED FLAG?

A Red Flag is a visual sign or indication of a defect in a structure or property.

Certain visual signs in themselves are not clear indications of defects, but if observed in multiple numbers, especially in the same approximate location, they probably point to the existence of a Red Flag condition. Safety hazards like other defects, are Red Flags and should be disclosed.

Because most property defects develop over a period of years, the age of the structure should be kept in mind during the inspection process. The broker or agent must evaluate the information obtained during the inspection relative to the age of the structure. Older structures (10 years or older) will show much more evidence of problems if problems exist, especially if maintenance has been neglected.

Very young structures (0 to 3 years old) pose a special problem. Not enough time has passed for the ongoing effects of a defect, if one should exist, to cause visible damage. Therefore, serious problems may be undetectable while a home is still young. If symptoms of distress are seen in a new home it is a sign of a possible severe and fast-moving defect.

Rule-of-thumb: Red Flags are much more worrisome if found in a new home and a lack of Red Flags is much more impressive in an old home.

RESEARCH AND PLANNING

Most brokers and agents are quite familiar with title reports, which usually include information on easements, property line distances and directions, and so on. County or city engineering departments usually keep copies of the original and any subsequent building or construction permits issued. In addition, copies of soil reports, engineering calculations, geologic reports, and other documents are also kept in city or county files.

When researching a property, always obtain all documents possible from the seller and review the title report or preliminary title report. If there is an indication of an illegal or non conforming addition, research city or county files for building permits. Any discrepancy or omission of information that comes to your attention during the research should be well documented for disclosure purposes.

A properly conducted Red Flags inspection consists of three parts: 1) the exterior of the building and the surrounding grounds, 2) the interior of the building, and appurtenant structures, including retaining walls and pools, tennis courts, and 3) environmental hazards.

Begin by inspecting the outside of the building and the surrounding grounds. Stop on the sidewalk and look at it with a critical eye. Note the slope of the land and general appearance of the house. Check for cracks in sidewalks, driveways, foundations, exterior walls, and fireplaces. Be alert for drainage problems, unstable soils, and unsafe conditions. Then take a closeup view of the surrounding property including hazardous trees and vegetation.

Go inside and inspect the interior of the home. Look for problems with floors, doors, windows, walls, stairways, and built-in systems such as the stove, furnace, fireplaces, and storage areas.

Lesson One

Inspect any appurtenant structures such as a pool, sauna, tennis court, guest house, or detached garage. Don't forget to inspect the appurtenant structures with as much care as the rest of the property and always inspect for any possible environmental hazards that may be present.

Refer to the illustrated inspection techniques in this course for step-by-step instructions.

WHAT ARE THE CAUSES FOR DAMAGE IN STRUCTURES?

This lesson deals with the most common conditions that may cause movement of a home. Such movement is usually differential in nature and causes damage evidenced by cracks in walls and foundations, sloping floors, sticking doors and windows, and so on.

No matter what the underlying cause of distress, the visual symptoms, or Red Flags, are generally the same. The exact source of damage, however, should be confirmed or determined by an expert.

EXPANSIVE SOILS

Expansive soils are a common problem in California, Texas, other southwestern states, and here and there throughout the country.

Expansive soils are composed mostly of clay. When exposed to water expansive soils will absorb the water and swell; in dry conditions they shrink. This swelling and shrinking can exert great force, and can easily move a relatively light structure such as a home.

If a new house is to be built on expansive soil, the soil type should be taken into consideration when the foundation is designed, or the house is likely to suffer damage from differential movement, especially in climates where a very dry season alternates with a wet season.

Expansive soils do not usually shrink and swell uniformly. In the Southwest, for example, the first winter rains following the long dry summer will start to saturate the soil around the perimeter of a home's foundation, but the water may not wet the soil under the house. As a result the outer walls of the building tend to rise up as the soil swells, while the inside portions remain stationary. This differential movement causes stress between different parts of the house, which often results in significant damage.

Expansive soils are usually black. dark brown, or dark red. When wet, they have a gooey texture and easily stick to the soles of shoes. When dry, they shrink and cracks appear on the ground that often form a hexagonal pattern, like the bottom of a dried-up pond.

Lesson One

If soil is black, soft, and sticky during the wet season, or if cracks appear on the ground in the dry season, the soil is probably expansive.

FILLS

Fill is soil that has been moved and placed artificially. Fills are most common in hillside developments, building tracts on level ground, and adjacent to bays, lakes, rivers, and marshes.

If soils are placed and compacted according to correct engineering criteria, they form a very dense material that is often nearly as hard as rock. Such fills are commonly used for earthen dams, canals, and building pads for structures. A well engineered and properly constructed fill is a good product and becomes an integral part of the foundation of a structure. Loose or "non-engineered fills," are poor products and are a major cause of structural damage.

Poor fills settle when they get wet or are subject to loading (as by the weight of a building). Vibrations, such as those from a nearby railroad, can also cause settling. Like expansive soils, fills do not usually move uniformly. The deepest, wet test, and loosest portions of the fill settle the most.

Fills are difficult for a lay person to detect. If terracing or unnatural slopes are seen, fills may have been used on the site and an effort should be made to determine whether they were properly engineered. If a distressed house is built on a fill, the fill is probably at least partly to blame for the damage.

FREEZING GROUND

In the northern portions of the United States and in Canada the ground freezes during the winter months. Actually, the soil itself does not freeze, the water held between soil particles freezes. Since water expands when it freezes and shrinks when it thaws, if structures built in frigid areas are not designed to withstand the pressure of freezing ground, their foundations may be subject to movement and damage.

If concrete slabs are improperly constructed, the corners and sides of the concrete can be lifted up by freezing ground, thereby distorting any structure built on the slab. This is why slab-on-grade construction is not common in freezing climates, and why basements are common in the northern states. Basements not only provide extra living and storage space, they also extend the home's foundation below the freeze level so that foundation movement is minimal. However, movement can still occur, especially if drainage next to the foundation is poor and water finds its way into the

Lesson One

basement. Damage caused by freezing ground is likely to occur within the first few years, and grows more and more severe each winter.

COLLAPSING SOILS, SINKHOLES, VOIDS

Sinkholes and voids come in many sizes and types. They are most common in Florida and parts of other southern states.

Every year, somewhere in the country, a house is reported to have fallen into a sinkhole. Such catastrophes are comparatively rare, but more slow moving and less dramatic cases are common. In Florida, for example, much of the soil is composed of carbonate particles that are slowly dissolved by ground and surface water. Small voids and large caverns develop beneath the earth, which can collapse and cause sinkholes.

Buried pipelines are commonly constructed by laying the lines in a trench and filling the trench with sand. If a water line ruptures in such a trench, especially on a hillside, the sand can be washed away, leaving a void. There would be no evidence of a problem until the surface actually collapsed and a sink hole occurred. Such an event would not necessarily be quick and dramatic; it could occur slowly, causing gradual settling of the ground surface and any structure built on it.

Silts are particularly common in the northern central states due to geologic processes that have occurred in the past. Such soils have the consistency of flour and are usually very loose. They can collapse when subjected to abundant water, heavy loads, or vibrations. Houses built on this kind of soil usually settle gradually but unevenly.

Soft clays are naturally deposited in bays, inlets, and lakes throughout the country. Peat deposits are common in the northern states. Both clay and peat will consolidate (compact) in time. The rate of consolidation can be accelerated by heavy loads. Thus, if a structure is built on such a deposit, damage can result. Consolidation tends to be a more generalized process than the differential movement caused by expansive soils and fills. The severity of damage is usually less than with other types of settlement, although similar Red Flag symptoms can be found.

LANDSLIDING

Landslides are quite common in the West, but can occur anywhere, mostly where steep slopes coupled with weak rock structure are prevalent. Most landslides occur when the ground is saturated with water and are, contrary to public impression, usually slow moving.

Lesson One

Landsliding is a specialized field of expertise reserved for engineering geologists and geotechnical engineers. Visual detection of landslides is usually difficult. Distress to a home can probably be observed, but the average real estate broker or agent will not usually be able to determine landsliding as the cause.

POOR DRAINAGE

Proper drainage of surface water near a structure is vital. If drainage is poor, water will pond next to the foundation and can seep under the structure or bleed through basement walls. The structure and its contents may be damaged. In addition, excessive amounts of water can aggravate existing soil conditions such as expansive soils, silts, or unstable fills. In cold climates, soil containing a high amount of water will swell most dramatically when frozen, possibly causing damage to the structure.

STRUCTURAL DEFECTS

Structural or construction defects are the underlying cause of distress in many properties. Undersized beams, improper nailing, and improper construction procedures in general cause defects in a structure. Such defects are usually very difficult to isolate. Where evidence of distress is observed and no specific causes can be identified, a structural or construction defect may be the reason. If there is any suspicion that a structural defect exists, a qualified civil or structural engineer should be retained for a detailed inspection.

Lesson One

LESSON ONE QUIZ

Answer the following questions based on the material contained in Lesson One.

1. What is a Red Flag?

    A. Something that is used to stop traffic
    B. A visual sign or indication of a defect in a structure or property
    C. Anything that causes a defect in a home
    D. A visual defect in a home for sale

2. The age of a home must be considered when evaluating Red Flags. A home less than four years old is considered "very young." A good rule of thumb to use when evaluating Red Flags and the age if a home is that

    A. Red Flags found in a very young home are not worrisome.
    B. a lack of Red Flags in a very young home is impressive.
    C. there is no correlation between the number of Red Flags and the age of a home.
    D. Red Flags are much more worrisome if found in a young home and the lack of Red Flags is much more impressive in an old home.

3. A proper inspection for Red Flags in a home should consist of three elements: 1) the inspection of the appurtenant structures to the home; 2) the inspection of the interior of the home; and 3) the inspection of

    A. the roof structure of the home.
    B. the exterior walls of the home.
    C. the exterior of the home and the surrounding ground.
    D. the condition of any other structures on the property.

4. One common condition that causes differential movement in a home is expansive soils. Expansive soils are composed mostly of

    A. loam.   B. clay.
    C. gravel.   D. carbonate particles.

5. A home built on expansive soil without the benefit of a properly engineered foundation design will suffer the greatest damage from differential movement in a climate where

    A. a very dry season alternates with a wet season.
    B. a very cold season alternates with a very warm season.
    C. the season is wet most of the time.
    D. the season is dry most of the time.

Lesson One

6. Expansive soils can be identified because

    A. they are light in color and are very slippery when wet.
    B. during the wet season they are black, firm, and sticky.
    C. during the dry season they are soft and fluffy in texture.
    D. they are black, soft, and sticky during the wet season, or cracks appear on the ground in the dry season.

7. "Fill soil" is defined as soil that has been excavated in one area, moved and placed artificially in another area. A structure that has been built on a "non-engineered" fill is subject to damage because

    A. the fill may settle when wet.
    B. settlement may occur because of the weight of the structure.
    C. None of the above
    D. All of the above

8. Freezing is another cause of structural damage to a home. The damage to the home is caused because

    A. the soil freezes.
    B. the water held between the soil particles expands and shrinks during freezing and thawing.
    C. All of the above
    D. None of the above

9. If drainage of surface water near a structure is not properly engineered, structural damage to a home can result from

    A. insect infestation.
    B. unsanitary conditions.
    C. ponding and aggravation of existing soil conditions.
    D. hydraulic pressures.

10. Where evidence of distress in a home is observed and no specific cause can be identified, the distress is usually caused by

    A. landsliding.
    B. sinkholes.
    C. structural defects.
    D. freezing ground.

LESSON TWO

INSPECTING FOR RED FLAGS OUTSIDE THE HOME

LEARNING OBJECTIVES

Upon completion of Lesson Two you will:

1. Understand the significance of cracks in structures, driveways, sidewalk, patios, and basement floors.

2. Learn the importance of proper drainage, building ventilation, hillside instability, and fills as well as the Red Flags associated with the problems created by the improper conditions related to these situations.

3. Be aware of the problems arising from roof, window, and flashing leakage and the Red Flags present.

4. Understand where the areas in and around a structure are that can contain possible defects and the Red Flags associated with these types of defects.

CRACKS IN SIDEWALKS, DRIVEWAYS AND DECKS

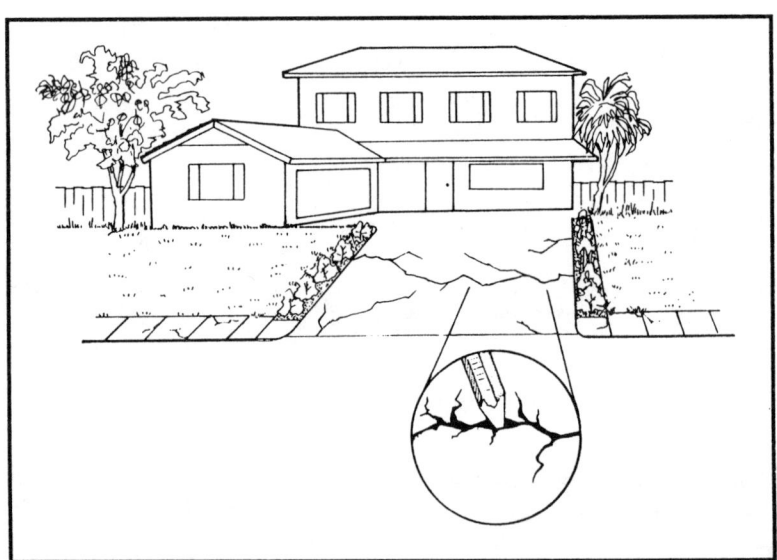

*Figure 2.1 Cracked driveway and sidewalks.
Some cracks show significant displacement.*

Most properties have asphalt or concrete driveways, sidewalks, patios, decks, slabs, or garage floors. It is important to check them for cracks and drainage.

A few hairline cracks are no cause for worry. However, cracks that are wide enough to insert a pencil tip can indicate a defect. If one side of a crack is raised enough to trip over, it is a safety hazard and an indication of uneven ground movement.

In general, large numbers of cracks, especially open or offset ones, should be considered as Red Flags. A few wide-open, or dramatically offset cracks are also Red Flags.

Inspect concrete stairways, decks, or patios constructed adjacent to the home's foundation. If they are on the downhill side of the building, the soil underneath them may be creeping down the hill. Look for cracks between the patio's edge and the home's foundation; if significant cracking is observed a possible Red Flag exists.

CRACKS IN FOUNDATIONS

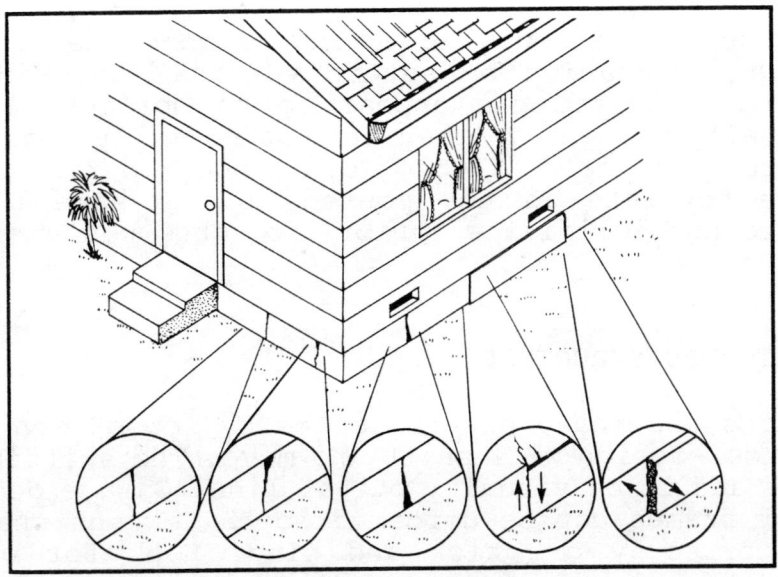

Figure 2.2 Common foundation cracks.

Cracks in foundations are common. They may indicate a severe problem or merely a normal condition of random cracking. A Red Flag exists if there is/are: 1) several severe cracks; 2) one crack showing a suspicious foundation movement; or 3) many hairline cracks, especially if clustered in one place.

Pole foundations are very difficult to inspect because most of the foundation is not visible. If a home has a pole foundation, pay special attention to symptoms of foundation distress like uneven floors, sticking doors, and cracked walls.

Lesson Two

To inspect an ordinary foundation, walk along the outside of the building, not more than five feet away from the foundation, and look for cracks.

Foundation cracks fall into several categories. Horizontal cracks are usually not serious, but you should note their location, width, and length. Vertical and diagonal cracks are more serious.

Hairline Cracks Hairline cracks look like pencil lines drawn on the surface. There are no openings between the edges. They do not usually indicate a serious problem unless a lot of hairline cracks are present, then they must be considered a possible Red Flag.

Open Cracks The width of open cracks should be estimated. Open cracks constitute a possible Red Flag, especially when one end of the crack is wider than the other. Be sure to measure the widest part of the crack.

Cracks with Vertical Slippage Vertical slipping may be very serious. It means that the concrete on one side of the crack has moved down. Cracks with vertical slippage constitute a Red Flag.

Horizontal Cracks Horizontal cracking of concrete foundations is almost always accompanied by severe vertical cracking. However, cold joints in concrete can appear to be horizontal cracks and although visually unsightly, they are not normally considered to be a serious structural defect. Cold joints occur during construction when all the concrete is not poured at the same time and the previous pouring solidifies prior to the placement of more concrete.

VISUALLY DISTORTED STRUCTURE

Structures that have been affected by foundation movement or structural under-design will shift and move. The shifting can cause walls to move and to be visually out of line. Garage doors or front and side door frames can be deformed to the extent that the doors do not fit correctly or stick and bind. Look for wall bulges, especially near the ground surface. Also look for cracking of the walls of the structure, particularly at the corners of windows and doors. Be sure to check for distorted door frames.

Minor or random hairline cracks have several possible causes and are not normally serious. Such cracking would not normally be a Red Flag. However, significant bulging of walls, out-of-square door frames, sticking doors, shimmed doors, or abundant cracking and cracking showing movements either vertical or horizontal should be considered a Red Flag.

Lesson Two   13

VISUALLY DISTORTED STRUCTURE

Figure 2.3 *This garage door frame has been distorted and is no longer rectangular*

DRAINAGE

Proper drainage of roof and yard areas is important, because water collecting near the home or underneath it can aggravate existing soil problems. Expansive soils, when exposed to a large volume of water, will swell to their maximum, then shrink dramatically when dried again. Many foundations cannot tolerate these maximum shrink/swell cycles, and cracking and settlement will result where these conditions exist. Loose fill and soil will sag and settle, causing damage if they are not kept well drained.

If water gathers in puddles right next to a foundation, it can easily seep under the home, causing basement flooding, wood rot, damage to heat ducts, and swelling of wood floors.

Lesson Two

DRAINAGE

Figure 2.4 *Uncontrolled roof water and poor surface drainage next to structure.*

Inspecting for Poor Drainage Imagine it is raining as you inspect the drainage systems, visualize water flowing through the system. Imagine where this water will end its journey.

Be alert for the following points during your inspection:

1. All water from the roof should be transported away from the structure usually through gutters and downspouts. Often closed pipes from the roof lead out to the driveway or the street, which keeps water from puddling next to the house.

2. Downspouts that empty next to the foundation or into planter boxes adjoining the home should be considered possible Red Flags.

3. The ground surface near the house should slope away from the building for at least the first few feet. Ground sloping toward a structure should be noted as a possible Red Flag.

4. Look for low spots next to structures where puddles could form. Ponds right next to the foundation of a house are a sign of poor drainage and constitute a possible Red Flag.

In general, good drainage exists if no water is allowed to pond or flow next to the home's foundation.

Lesson Two

BUILDING VENTILATION

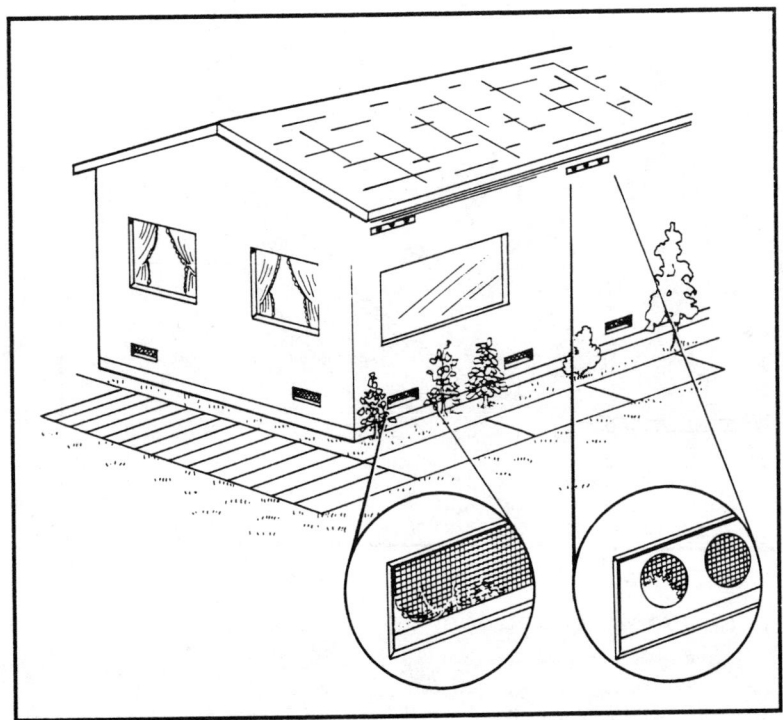

Figure 2.5   Damaged ventilation screens in crawl space and attic.

In many parts of the country adequate ventilation is designed into structures as depicted above. The ventilation portals are screened to prevent the entrance of rodents and insects. The integrity of the ventilation portals should be inspected and any damage reported.

HILLSIDE INSTABILITY, LANDSLIDING

A hillside is stable if it is likely to remain in its present form, at rest, without sliding or eroding. The average real estate broker or agent does not have the expertise to recognize most landslides. It is difficult for even an expert to predict the future stability of a hillside. However, an inspection can be made for signs of past instability, erosion, or soil sloughage.

Landslides (mass movement of soil and rock) move at various speeds. Some move very slowly and may slide only a few inches before stopping. If a home is built on an active landslide, differential movement of the structure may have occurred. This often causes foundation cracks, wall cracks, and sloping floors.

Lesson Two   16

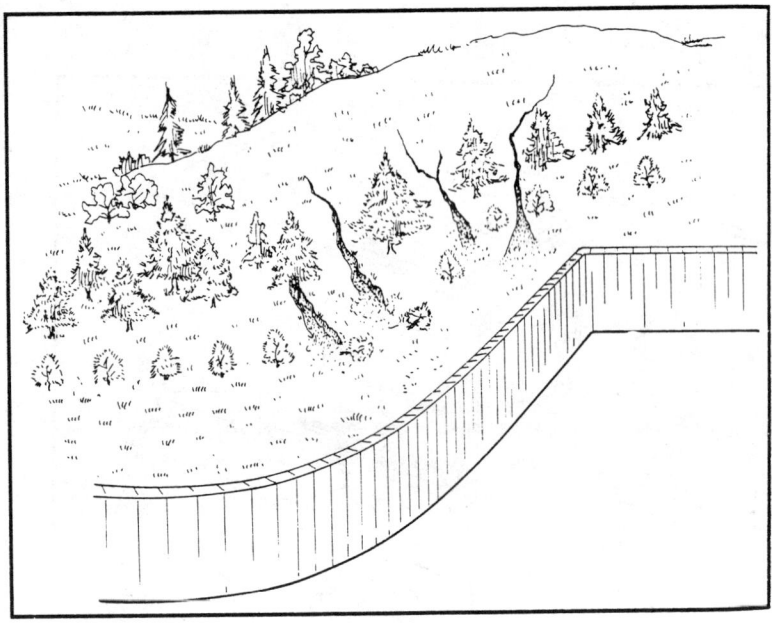

Figure 2.6   Erosion features on hillside.

Plastic sheets covering areas of a hillside may indicate a Red Flag. Bowl-shaped depressions on a hillside may also indicate past instability or soil sloughage.

Small-scale landslides are often repaired with retaining walls. Usually several walls are built, like steps going up the slope. If there are several retaining walls on the property, ask the homeowner why they were built.

FILLS

Figure 2.7   Filled building pad.

Lesson Two 17

   Most hillside homesites as well as many level homesites have varying amounts of fill--soil used to fill low areas of a site, which creates a flat pad on which to build. Fill may have been used on only a few small dips and gullies; or, if the site was originally quite steep, a great deal of fill may have been used.

It is difficult to determine by visual inspection alone whether fills exist and whether the fill was constructed correctly. However, improper fills may make their presence known by the damage they cause.

Fills on the downhill edges of driveways, patios, and other slabs often move down the hill and away from the house, unfortunately taking any asphalt or concrete along with them. This movement is called "creep." The effect on asphalt driveways tends to be a series of cracks parallel to the driveway's edge. Minor amounts of creep are to be expected in hillside areas, but large or wide cracks in driveways, patios, and walkways can indicate a serious problem, and must be considered a Red Flag.

Fills underneath the house can settle, causing foundation cracks, wall cracks, and sticking doors and windows.

ROOF, WINDOW, AND FLASHING LEAKAGE

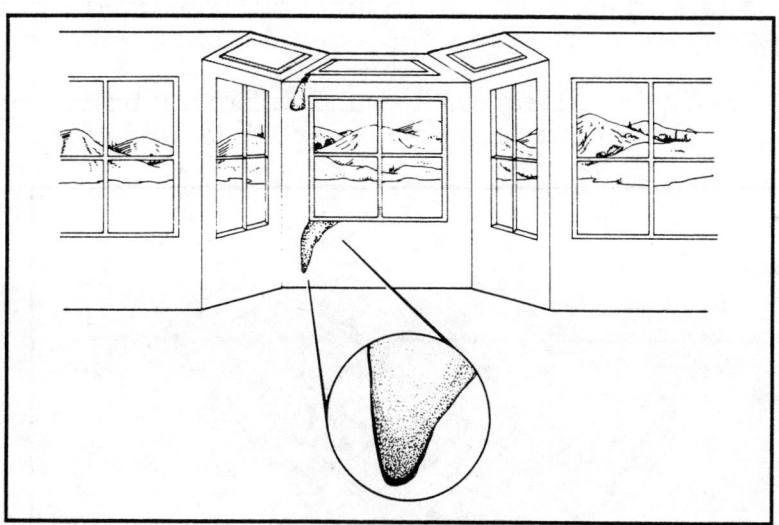

Figure 2.8   Wall and window stains.

   A leaking roof is a major problem and is often very expensive to repair, especially if the roof needs to be completely replaced. If there are any signs of roof leakage, a licensed general

Lesson Two   18

contractor or roofing contractor should be called in to do an inspection.

Window or flashing leakage in a home constitutes a serious problem and can cause significant damage if not detected. The most common sign of past leakage is wood and wall staining. Any evidence of roof, window, or flashing leakage constitutes a Red Flag.

Look for the following Red Flags on roofs:

- Green moss or other growth signify a possible moisture or wood rot problem. Tree branches or plants in contact with the roof could also cause problems.

- If the home has a shingle roof, look for missing shingles. If the shingles are curling up and separating, the roof may be old--get a roof inspection.

- Deteriorated flashing.

- On composition tile roofs, erosion of mineral coating.

- On tar and gravel roofs, blisters and erosion of gravel.

- Holes and curls in shakes.

- Water stains and wet areas in attics, on windows or ceilings indicate that roof leakage has been in progress for some time.

- If areas on the ceiling or around windows have recently been painted over, there may be water stains underneath.

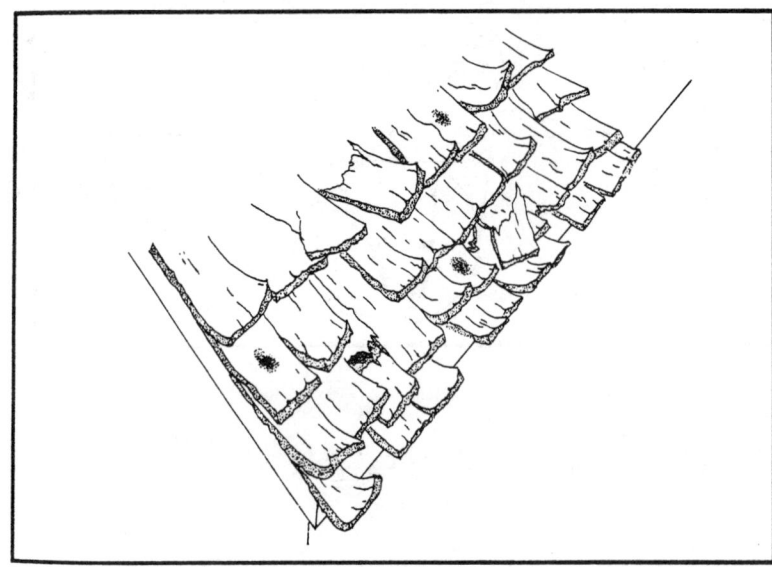

Figure 2.9   Deteriorated shake roof.

Lesson Two

LIFE EXPECTANCY OF ROOFING

Fire Rating	Type of Roof	Life Expectancy
Class "A"	Spanish Tile	50 years
	Light Weight Cement	50 years
	Aluminum Shake	50 years
	Composition Tile	20 years
	Tar and Gravel	15 years
Class "C"	Cedar Shingle	25 years
	Wood Shake	20-25 years

HAZARDOUS VEGETATION

Figure 2.10   Foundation damaged and cracked by root system.

Lesson Two

20

Check around the house for trees or bushes that could cause damage. These include good-sized trees or bushes less than 5 feet from the side of the house, and very large trees up to 15 feet away. The roots of large trees and bushes can grow under the foundation. patio, driveway, or sidewalks, breaking the concrete with their roots. They can also dry out soils by simply drinking up all the water.

Among the most common hazards are dead or unhealthy trees. Dead trees are dangerous because they are unstable and moderate winds can often topple them, causing major damage to structures, not to mention the possibility of injury to the building's occupants. Dead or unhealthy trees should be identified, especially those close to habitable structures.

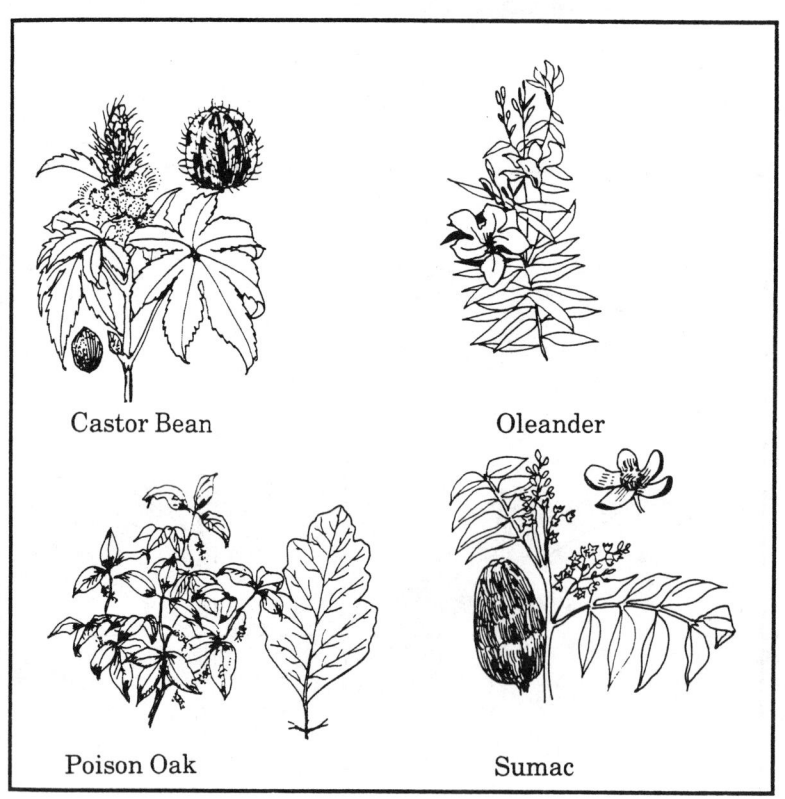

Figure 2.11   Examples of hazardous vegetation.

Poisonous plants--many of which are common in landscaping--can cause health problems. Poison oak, poison sumac, poison ivy, castor bean, mulberry bushes, and so on, located near the home should be documented and disclosed.

Lesson Two

HAZARDOUS RAILINGS

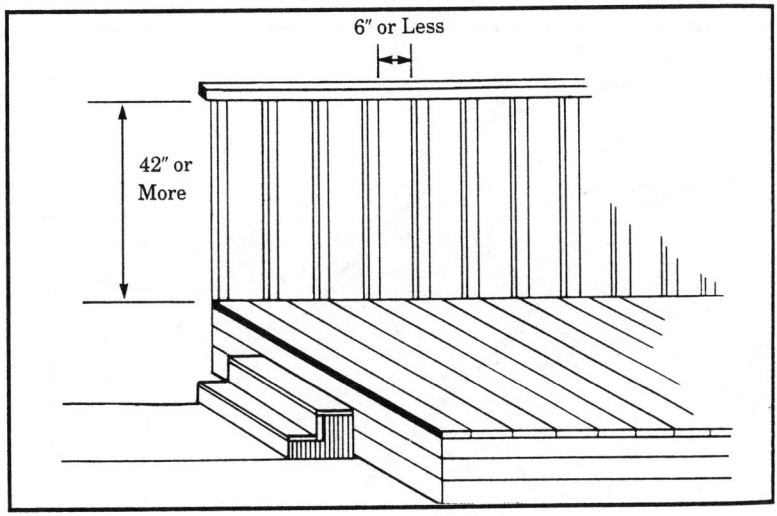

Figure 2.12   Typical deck railings and steps.

(Some measurements of specific house components are given in this guide to assist the broker or agent in determining during the visual inspection if significant variations from the norm exist. Significant variations from normal measurements as presented herein may indicate code violations, illegal additions or possible safety hazards.)

Deck, porch, and balcony railings need to be inspected. According to the Uniform Building Code (UBC Secs. 1711,3306), all decks 30 inches or more above the ground require railings, which should be a minimum of 42 inches high (or 36" per exception) on residential property, and the gaps between rails should be no more than six inches.

Improperly braced railings can be a significant safety hazard. Pots or planters precariously located on railings can also be hazardous. Handrails are required for all steps with four or more risers. They should be 32 to 34 inches above stair treads. Any identified safety hazard should be disclosed.

Lesson Two   22

HAZARDOUS STAIRS

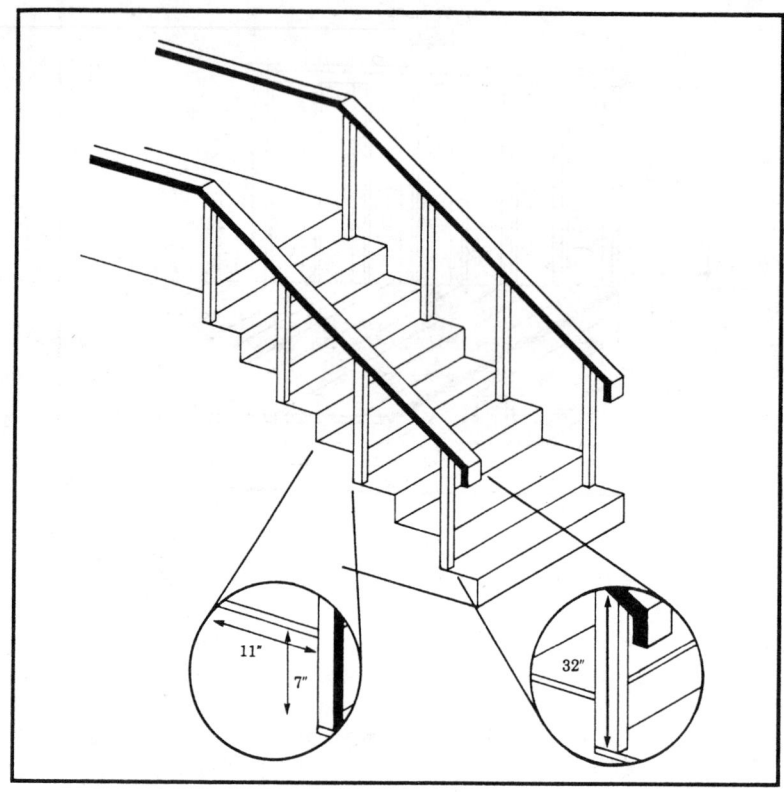

Figure 2.13   Typical stairway with normal railings.

     Improper rise and tread depth on stairs can cause accidents and are safety hazards. Risers should be 7 or 8 inches at most. Treads should equal 11 inches with no more than a 3/8 inch variation (UBC Sec. 3306j).

Lesson Two   23

HAZARDOUS WALKWAYS AND STEPS

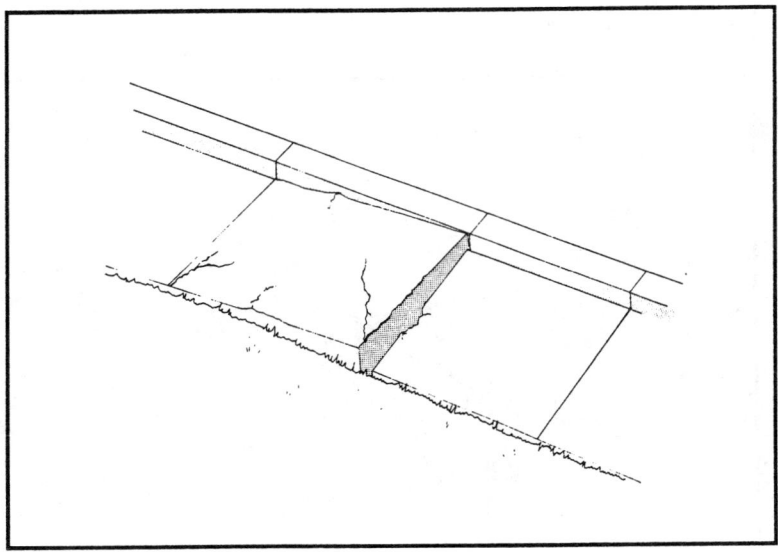

Figure 2.14   Hazardous Walkway.

Broken walkways or steps, including but not limited to offset concrete slabs, settled steps, missing boards in steps or decks, and rotten boards, all pose safety hazards (UBC Sec. 104d).

SEPTIC SYSTEMS

Properties with septic systems (buried sewage disposal systems) should be checked for system malfunction. Indications of a malfunctioning system include a strong sewage smell or discolored water ponding near the location of the disposal system.

GARAGE DOOR SPRINGS

Garage door springs are designed with a wire or cable through the center so that if the spring shatters, pieces do not fly through the air like bullets. If no such wire or cable exists, a safety hazard exists.

RETAINING WALLS

Retaining walls are used to hold soil that would otherwise slide down. They are built of wood, rock, concrete, etc. Most retaining walls should last 100 years or longer. However, untreated wood or Douglas fir walls only last 10 to 20 years before they decay due to wood rot.

Lesson Two   24

A retaining wall is not supposed to move or crack. It is should have a drainage system to keep water from building up behind the wall and pushing it forward.

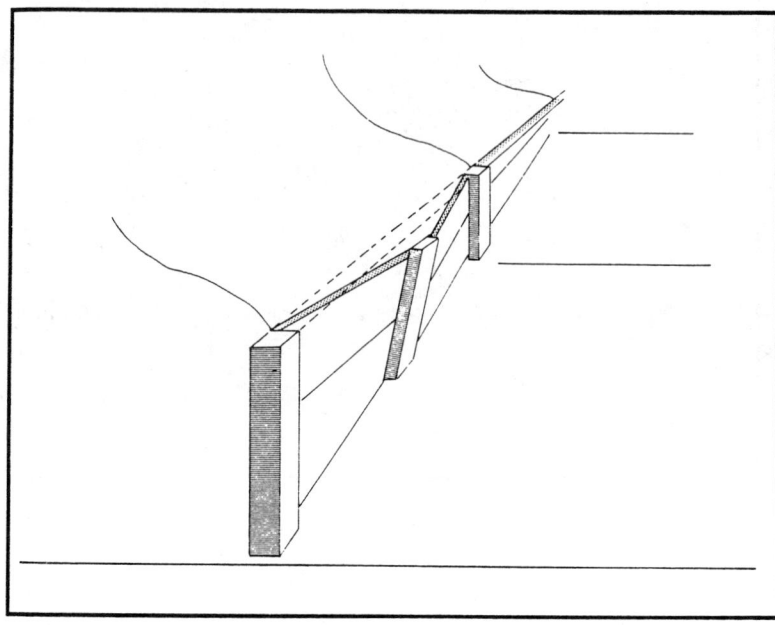

Figure 2.15   Failing retaining wall.

Inspection Procedure:

1. Stand up against the wall at one end. Look down the length of the wall to see if the top of the wall is leaning away from the hillside. Repeat this at each end of the retaining wall.

2. Walk along the length of the retaining wall, staying no farther than five feet away. Look for cracks, especially those that show movement.

3. Check for proper drainage. A drainage system may consist of holes in the lower portion of the wall ("weep holes"), or spaces between boards of wood. Signs of poor drainage are: 1) large water stains, or 2) collections of fuzzy crystals (whitish powder) on the front of the wall. Any evidence of improper drainage or the lack of drainage relative to the retaining walls is a possible Red Flag.

Any severe cracking or tilting of a retaining wall indicates possible failure and constitutes a Red Flag.

Lesson Two

SWIMMING POOLS AND SPAS

Figure 2.16   Swimming pool showing out-of-level water surface relative to coping.

Check for levelness: Measure the distance from the rim of the pool to the surface of the water. The water should be within 1/2 inch of the same level all around the pool. If it is not, a problem may exist. If the pool is built on a hill, and the water level is much lower on the uphill side than on the down hill side, it is possible the pool has tilted. This condition is definitely a Red Flag.

The sides and bottom of the pool should be sound and free from cracks. Many pools have experienced some concrete shrinkage during construction; therefore, one or two hairline or minor cracks are common. If an open crack is observed, a problem exists and a professional pool inspection would be appropriate.

Inspect the decks around the pool for cracks with the same method used for patio slabs or sidewalks.

TENNIS COURTS

Tennis courts are usually concrete or asphalt constructed over a base of crushed rock and dense or compacted soils. It is important for the court to be in good condition, because it is a valuable asset.

Lesson Two

Tennis courts should be slightly higher in the center than on the sides, so water can drain off. Water should not form puddles on the court.

Both asphalt and concrete tennis courts should be inspected for cracks and settlement in the same manner used for driveways.

Short cracks pointing in random directions could merely mean the asphalt is aging and has not been maintained. Longer cracks, particularly open ones, could be caused by expansive soils or settlement of fills.

PLAY STRUCTURES

Play structures for children, such as tree houses or elaborate swing systems in trees, can be quite hazardous. If a tree house is on a property, its safety should be checked.

ILLEGAL ADDITIONS

Figure 2.17   Common illegal addition.

Illegal additions to homes are a very common problem. Many such additions are built without a permit, and quite often the electrical, plumbing, and other elements are not safe or built to code. Illegal additions are Red Flags.

Lesson Two

LESSON TWO QUIZ

Answer the following questions based on the material contained in Lesson Two.

1. All of the following types of cracks in a concrete driveway, sidewalk, patio, or garage floor are Red Flags EXCEPT

    A. cracks that are open enough to insert a pencil tip.
    B. several hairline cracks.
    C. significant cracking between a patio's edge and the home's foundation.
    D. a few wide open or dramatically offset cracks.

2. Cracks in foundations are common. They may indicate a normal condition or a severe problem. A Red Flag exists if one of three conditions is present: 1) if there is one crack showing a suspicious foundation movement; 2) if there are many hairline cracks, especially if clustered in one place; and 3) if

    A. there is one horizontal hairline crack.
    B. there is a crack in a mortar joint.
    C. there are several severe cracks.
    D. there is a uniform crack between the slab floor and the foundation wall.

3. To properly inspect an ordinary foundation, you should walk along the outside of the foundation looking for cracks at a distance of not more than

    A. three feet.   B. five feet
    C. seven feet.   D. nine feet

4. A visually distorted structure is a structure that

    A. presents an unappealing architectural image.
    B. has been affected by adverse weathering conditions.
    C. has been affected by deferred maintenance.
    D. has been affected by foundation movement.

5. Generally, good drainage exists if

    A. water gathers in puddles next to the foundation.
    B. the ground surface adjacent to the home slopes toward the foundation.
    C. no water is allowed to pond or flow next to the home's foundation.
    D. water from downspouts flow into planter boxes adjoining the home.

Lesson Two

6. You are inspecting a property prior to taking a listing and notice that in the side yard there are several retaining walls built like steps going up the slope. You should

    A. include in your inspection report that the property is subject to landslides.
    B. say nothing because they might be a part of the overall landscaping.
    C. ask the home owner why they were built.
    D. refuse the listing.

7. When inspecting a home built on a "FILL" the term "creep" refers to

    A. movement.
    B. movement of patios, driveways, and other slabs on the uphill side of the home.
    C. movement of patios, driveways, and other slabs on the downhill side of the home.
    D. the vertical distance of travel.

8. You are inspecting a property prior to taking a listing and notice that there are signs of roof leakage, you should

    A. include in you inspection report that the property is subject to roof leakage.
    B. say nothing because the owner can paint over the stains.
    C. point out the problem and suggest that a licensed general contractor or a roofing contractor should be called in to do an inspection.
    D. tell the owner to get the roof fixed.

9. When inspecting a property, particular attention should be paid to good sized trees or bushes that are

    A. less than eleven feet from the side of the house.
    B. less than nine feet from the side of the house.
    C. less than seven feet from the side of the house.
    D. less than five feet from the side of the house.

10. Deck, porch, and balcony railings should be inspected. According to the Uniform Building Code (UBC Secs. 1711,3306) all decks, porches, and balconies must have a railing if they are

    A. 12 inches but less than 18 inches above the ground.
    B. 18 inches but less than 24 inches above the ground.
    C. 24 inches but less than 30 inches above the ground.
    D. 30 inches or more above the ground.

LESSON THREE

INSPECTING FOR RED FLAGS INSIDE THE HOME

LEARNING OBJECTIVES

Upon completion of Lesson Three you will:

1. Be aware of and learn to pay special attention to the several areas inside the home that can contain Red Flags.

2. Learn the procedures for detecting Red Flags in areas of the home such as floors, doors and windows, fireplaces, stairways, and glass panes.

3. Learn possible locations for concealed Red Flags and be aware of the reasons for concealment.

4. Understand what major mechanical systems in a home are and learn where to look for Red Flags in each of the systems.

BASEMENTS AND CRAWL SPACES

The same method used for inspecting foundations should be used for inspecting basement walls. Walk along the basement walls no further than five feet away from the foundation, using a strong flashlight, and note the type, location, and angle of any cracks.

Be alert for white, powdery deposits along foundations and walls, especially if there are also water stains. These are mineral deposits (calcium carbonates and calcium sulfates), an indication of repeated occurrences of moisture seepage in the basement or crawl space. Look for a "sump pump" in the lowest part of the basement floor. If there is one, it most likely had to be installed as a result of incoming water. Always ask the owners if water ever accumulated in the basement or crawl space.

If evidence of significant and abnormal moisture conditions is observed, a possible Red Flag condition exists. The existence of a sump pump or previous flooding constitutes a Red Flag and should be appropriately disclosed.

Lesson Three

WALL CRACKS

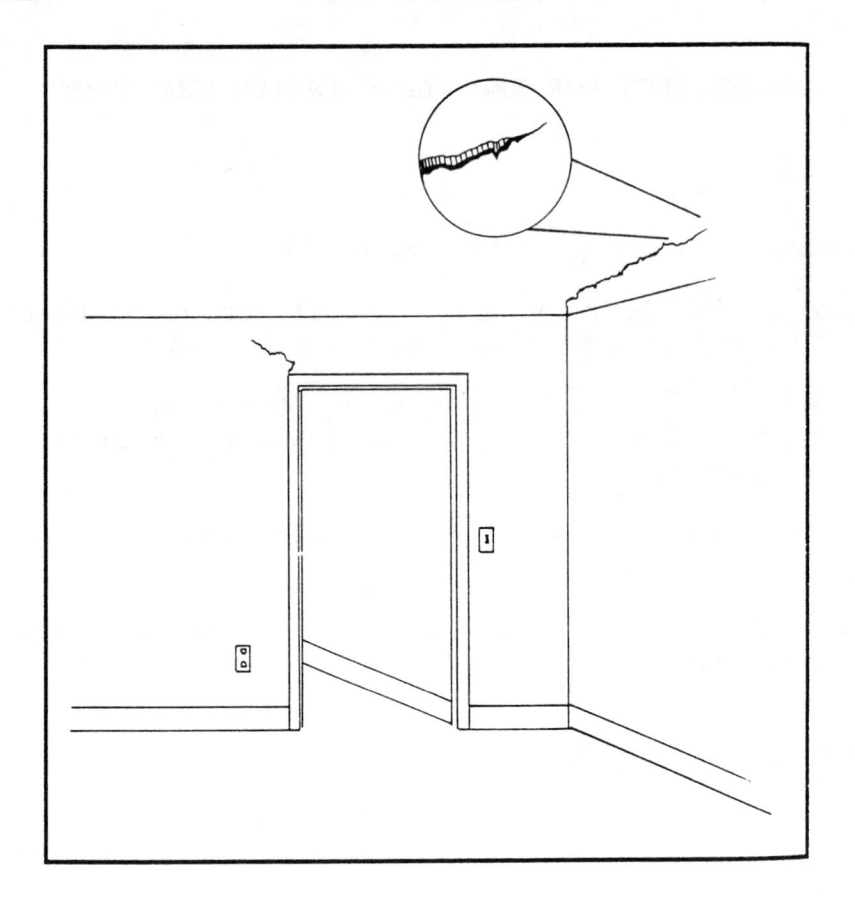

Figure 3.1   Wall and ceiling cracks.

Cracks develop in the walls of houses for a number of reasons. For instance, the wooden framing of the house may dry out and shrink shortly after the house is built. Almost every home has a few hairline cracks, caused by shrinkage of wood. However, differential movement of the structure may occur, caused by foundation movement, or structural defect which can cause significant wall cracking.

When inspecting inspect for cracking, pay particular attention to common crack locations such as the corners of windows, doors, and rooms. Consciously look for cracks behind curtains and on ceilings throughout the house and make written notes of the amount and severity of any cracking observed. Where significant amounts of cracks of large magnitude exist, serious distress to the home may have occurred, and indicate a Red Flag condition.

Small hairline cracks at the corners of a few windows or doors without other indications of possible distress to the home would not normally be considered a Red Flag. However, significant amounts

Lesson Three 31

of cracking or large cracks showing off-set or spaces should be considered a Red Flag. Minor cracking or hairline cracking associated with other indications such as sloping floors or sticking windows or doors would, in combination, be considered a Red Flag.

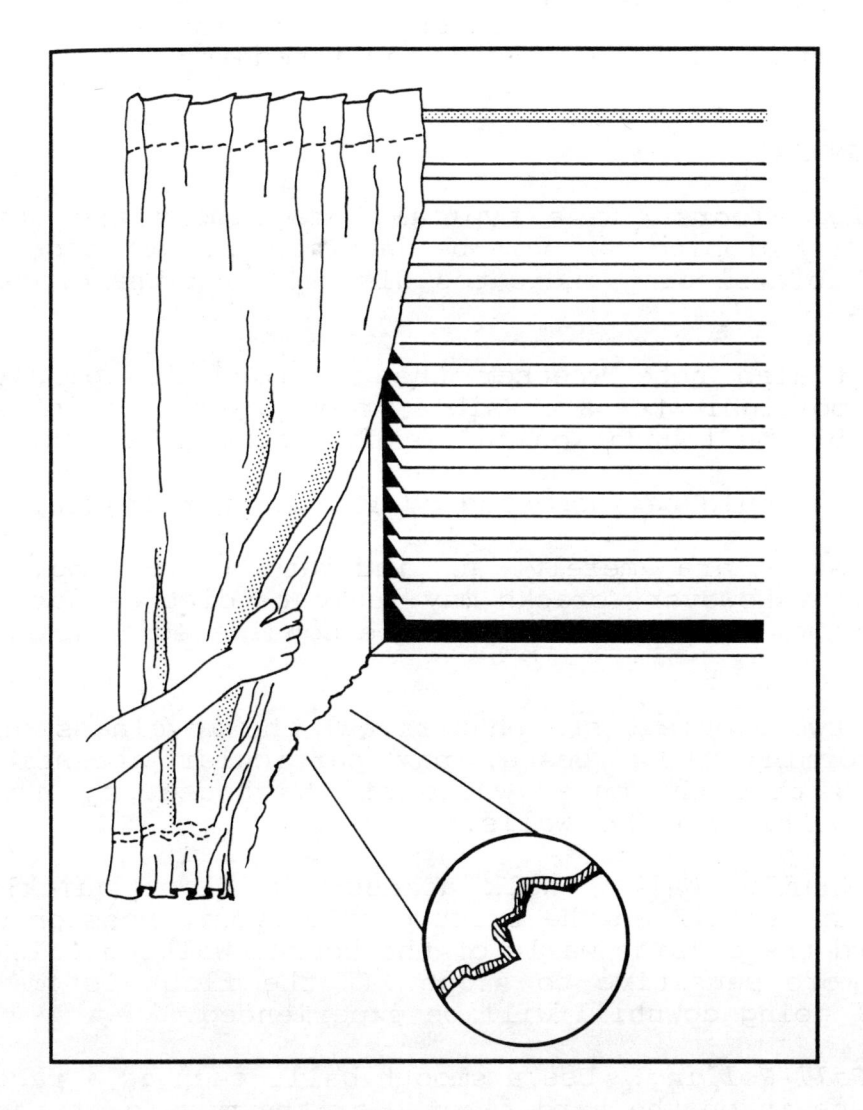

Figure 3.2   Hidden wall crack.

CONCEALED RED FLAGS

Home owners commonly paint and patch homes for aesthetic reasons prior to selling them. However, often they inadvertently conceal or hide indications of defects (Red Flags). Therefore, the Broker and Agent should make an effort to determine if Red Flags have been concealed. The most common types of Red Flags that are concealed include: wall cracks, wall stains, sticking doors and windows.

Lesson Three

Often a patched wall area will have a different surface texture from the rest of the wall. The color of the paint may also be slightly off. Where wallpaper has been used to redecorate walls, cracks can be concealed. However, often the cracks can be felt with the fingertips. In general, where the existence of hidden or concealed Red Flags is suspected, the inspection should be conducted with even more caution and intensity.

HOUSE ALIGNMENT

Sloping Floors In a typical home floors are sufficiently level and any sloping can only be determined by precise measuring. Any noticeable sloping indicates distress and therefore is a Red Flag.

You should also note whether the floors feel springy. A very springy floor indicates a possible problem with the interior floor structure or the foundation and is therefore a Red Flag.

Tile floors should be inspected by looking for cracks.

Often, cracks are merely an indication of improper floor construction. However, cracks may indicate distress especially if other symptoms exist. These should be considered as a possible Red Flag.

There are two simple tests that reveal the levelness of a floor. When performing these tests, pay particular attention to the possibility that the outer walls of the house may have settled relative to the interior walls.

Test #1--Shuffle Walk: Walk across the floor quickly without lifting your feet. Keep the front part of your shoes on the floor. Move toward the outside walls of the house. Walking this way makes you much more sensitive to slope. If the floor is not level, a feeling of going downhill will be experienced.

Test #2--Ball-Rolling: Use a smooth ball, such as a racquet ball. First, place it on the hard floor near the middle of the room and see if it rolls. Then try placing the ball in several spots around the room. If the ball rolls to the same spot repeatedly, that spot must be lower than the rest of the floor. Any evidence of sloping should be noted as a Red Flag.

Sticking Doors and Windows There are two things to look for when inspecting doors and windows: 1) sticking when they are opened and closed, and 2) uneven spaces between doors and their frames. These two symptoms usually mean the shape of the window or door frame has been changed by movement of the walls and floors.

Lesson Three   33

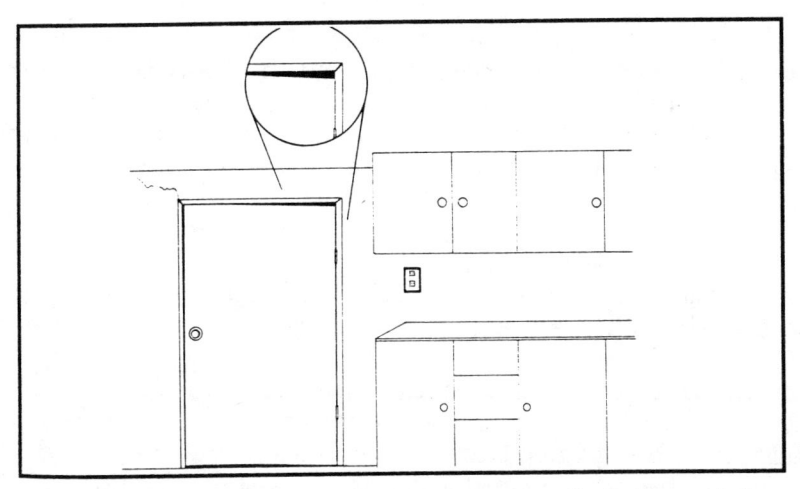

Figure 3.3   Out-of-square door frame with cracking.

All doors and windows in the house should be opened and closed to determine if they are sticking. This includes doors of cupboards and cabinets in the kitchen and bathrooms. If sticking occurs, determine the point where the door or window is rubbing against the frame.

Inspecting a door To inspect a door, look at the spaces at the top and bottom. The width of the space should be the same at the right and left sides, shaped like a long narrow rectangle and not a triangle. Uneven spaces usually mean the door frame has been distorted and is no longer a rectangle, while the door itself has not changed shape. Also look for signs that the door has been sawed or sanded to make it fit the crooked frame.

If doors and windows do not open and close easily, if unusual spaces are seen, or if there are signs of sanding, a note should be made of which door and exactly what seems to be wrong with it.

FIREPLACES

Figure 3.4   Cracked fireplace and poor roof damage.

Lesson Three

   Most fireplace structures are much heavier than the house structure (on a pounds-per-square-foot basis) and may settle, even if the home does not. Settling may cause a few hairline cracks where the edge of the fireplace meets the wall, but these usually are not serious.

Stand three to five feet away from the fireplace and inspect it from top to bottom, from both inside and outside the home. Be sure to pull away the hearth screen and inspect inside the fireplace.

Most codes require a fire-resistant hearth in front of a fireplace for a distance of 18 inches. Often the hearth is constructed of the same material as the fireplace, (bricks, stone, and so on). The absence of such a hearth constitutes a safety hazard.

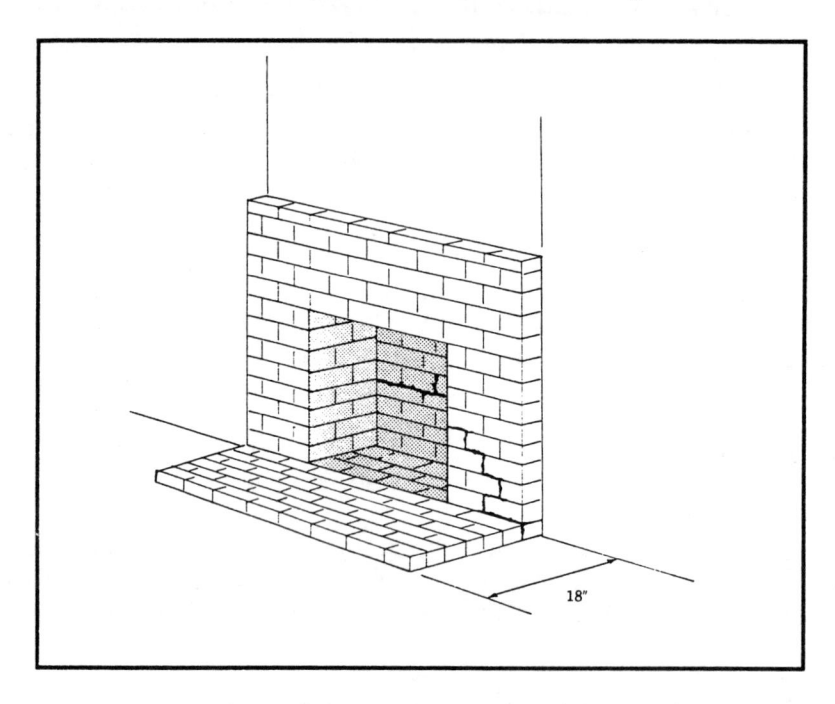

Figure 3.5   Cracks in fireplace and fire brick.

If severe settling has occurred, cracks may appear between the bricks, or diagonally through the bricks. Significant cracking constitutes a Red Flag. Open cracks in a fireplace can be a very serious safety hazard and must be considered a Red Flag. If cracks in the fireplace, especially in the fire box, are observed, an appropriate expert should inspect it. Such cracks can be a significant fire hazard.

Lesson Three

SAGGING BEAMS

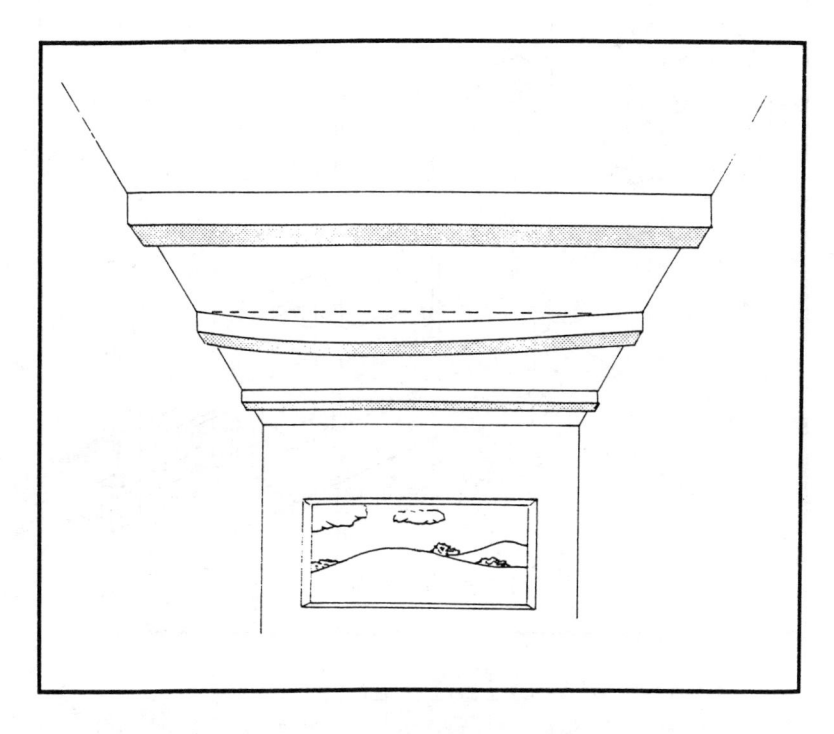

Figure 3.6   Sagging beam.

If portions of a building are improperly sized, the wrong building materials are used, or proper construction methods are not followed, distress to a home can occur. It is normally beyond the ability of a broker or agent to detect such problems. However, there are a few obvious symptoms, such as sagging beams, that may be seen in the course of a visual inspection.

Sagging beams can be easily detected especially if they are so much lower in the middle that the unevenness can be seen with the naked eye. In milder cases, there may be cracks where the beam connects to the framing of the house. These conditions should be disclosed as possible Red Flags and an inspection by a civil engineer or contractor may be recommended.

MAJOR MECHANICAL SYSTEMS

Common major house systems are electrical, plumbing, heating, and air conditioning.

Electrical System Check for damaged and malfunctioning receptacles and wall switches. Look for burn or scorch marks. Extension cords underneath carpets and cords stapled along baseboards are hazardous and illegal. Such conditions are Red Flags.

Lesson Three 36

Figure 3.7   Burned electrical outlet.

The Uniform Building Code and most state and local codes prohibit exposed wiring of many types in homes and garages. If exposed wiring is observed, a possible Red Flag exists and an inspection by an electrician may be recommended.

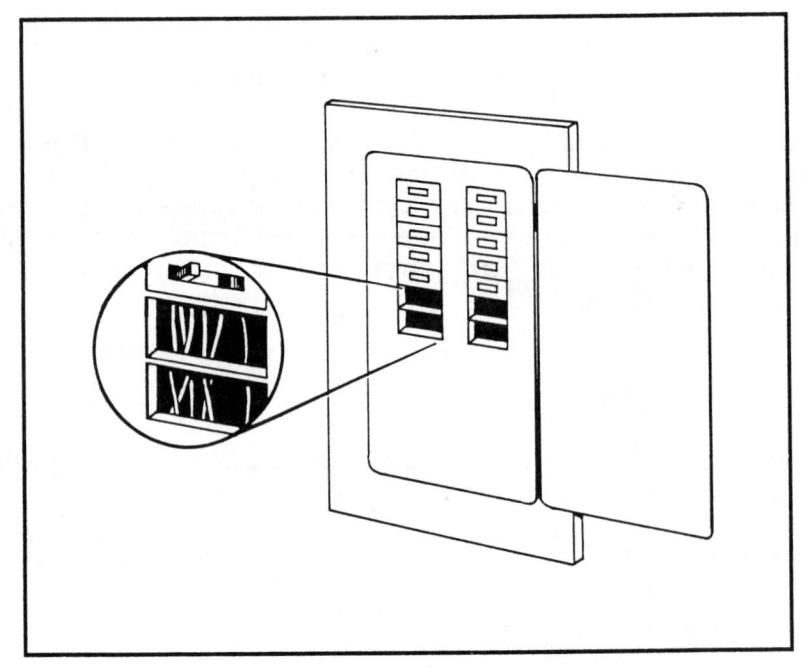

Figure 3.8   Electrical panel with openings (code violation).

Lesson Three

Electrical panels should be accessible for electrical shutdown purposes. Furniture or debris blocking access to the electrical panel constitutes a safety hazard. Panels with holes or knocked out plates are hazardous and a safety hazard.

A relatively new development in shock prevention, the Ground Fault Interrupter (GFI), is a special electrical outlet (plug-in unit) that acts as a circuit breaker. It shuts off the circuit so fast that a hazardous current never develops. GFIs are advisable as a safety precaution for all outlets near sinks and bathtubs. Many codes require GFI outlets for pools, spas, exterior receptacles, bathrooms, bar sinks and garages. The absence of GFI outlets near sinks and bathtubs should be noted as Red Flags.

Turn all light switches, built-in electrical appliances such as the stove, dishwasher, and laundry facilities on and off. This is not required as part of the inspection, but it is advisable and prudent.

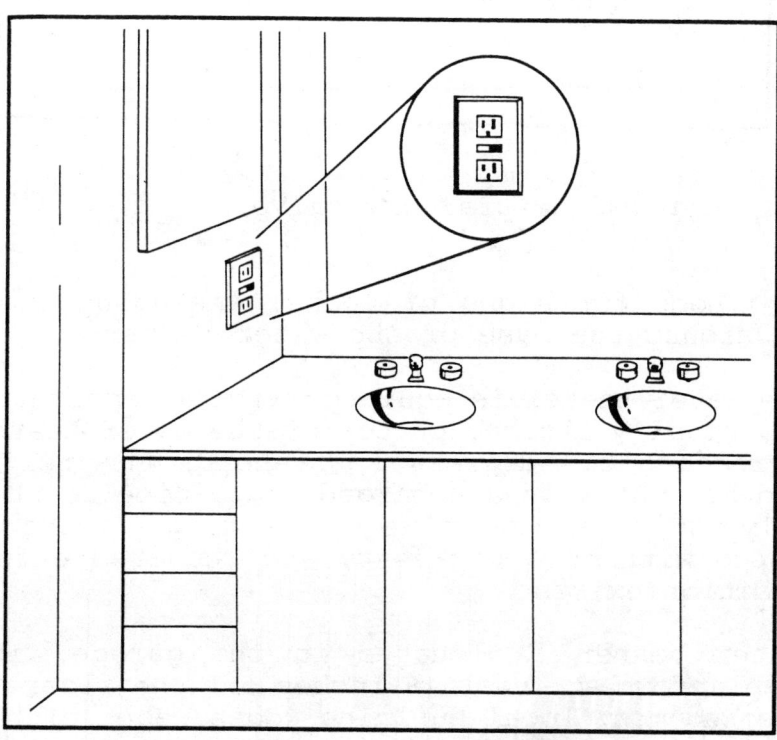

Figure 3.9   Typical ground fault interrupter (GFI).

Plumbing System Flush all toilets. Turn on all water taps. Do they dip when turn off? If the water source is a private well, have the nearest water district test water samples for safety.

Gas and electric shutoffs must be accessible for quick and easy turnoff. Blocked or inaccessible gas valves or electric switches are Red Flags.

Lesson Three

Figure 3.10   Typical natural gas valve.

Water Heater Look for signs of leaks, including rust and water spots at and around the base of the water heater.

Make sure the water heater is equipped with a temperature/pressure relief valve, usually located on top of the water heater. When the temperature reaches 210 degrees Fahrenheit, the relief valve is activated and hot water is discharged via a pipe to the outside. A lever manually activates the valve for testing. If the water heater is not equipped with this necessary and required safety device a Red Flag condition exists.

If a gas water heater is located in the garage, it should be mounted on a platform at least 18 inches off the floor. The Uniform Building Code and most local building codes require that the pilot flame of a water heater in a garage or carport be a minimum of 18 inches from the floor of the garage, to minimize the chance of gasoline fumes building up near the floor and being ignited by the water heater pilot light. This is a very important safety factor; the location and general condition of water heaters should be checked during a property inspection.

In many states water heaters are required to be secured by a seismic strap, a metal or fabric belt that holds the water heater erect in the event of an earthquake. Many jurisdictions require energy blankets on water heaters to minimize heat loss.

Lesson Three 39

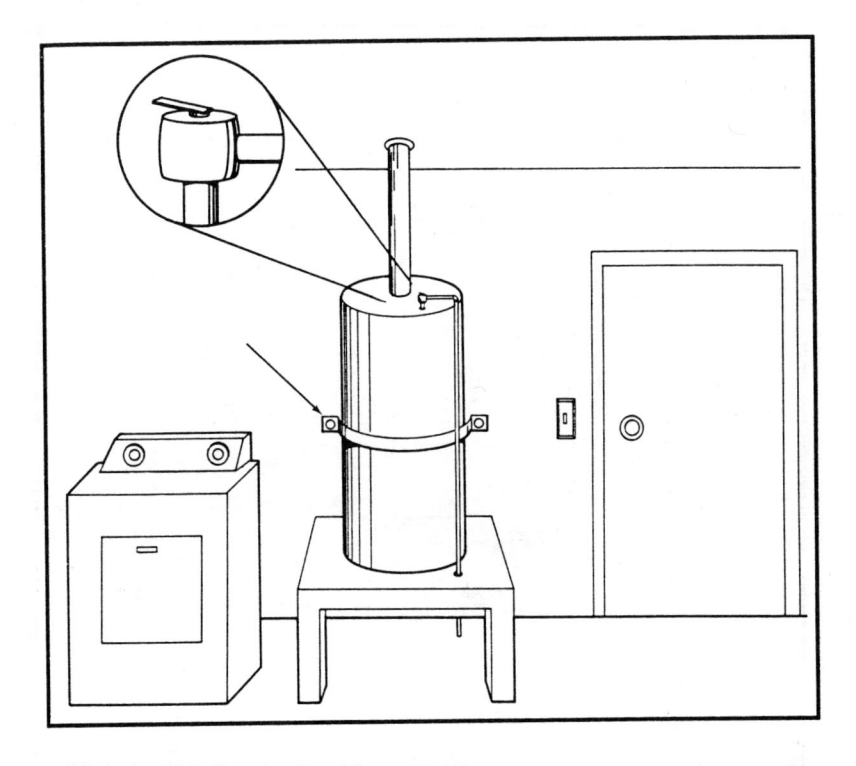

Figure 3.11 Water heater in garage. Note 18 inch pedestal and pressure relieve valve.

The absence of proper ventilation for water heaters and furnaces can be a serious hazard. Such ventilation requirements are relatively technical in nature. However, if no ventilation is apparent, a possible Red Flag condition exists.

Heating, Air Conditioning Turn the thermostat up and down to see if heat or cool air comes on quickly and the system operates quietly. It is a good idea to have the heating system on while inspecting the electrical appliances, then turn on the air conditioner while inspecting the plumbing fixtures.

STAIRWAYS

Improperly constructed stairs, with undersized steps that have a larger or smaller than normal rise or single steps between rooms could pose a tripping hazard and are possible Red Flags. Such abnormal stairs and steps are an indication of an illegal addition. Risers should be 7 or 8 inches at most. Threads should equal 11 inches with no more than a 3/8 inch variation.

Lesson Three

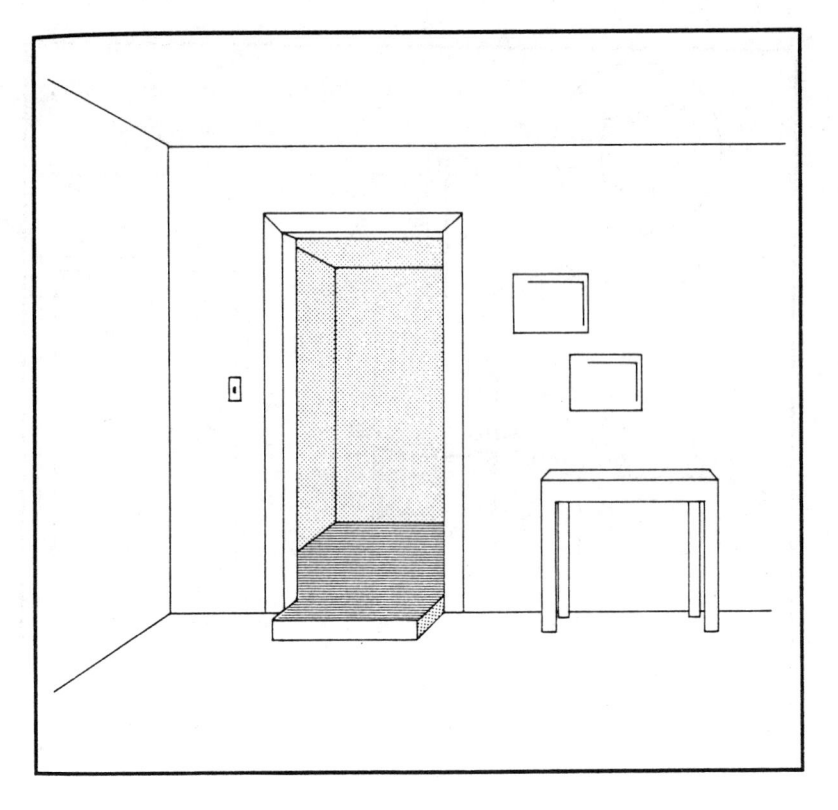

Figure 3.12   Hazardous step.

GLASS

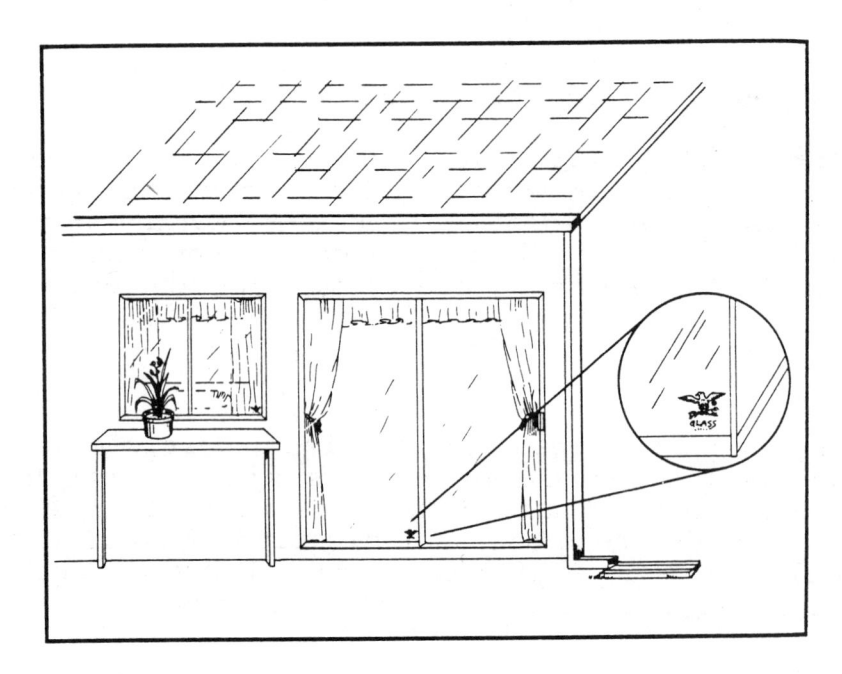

Figure 3.13   Typical safety glass decal on sliding glass door.

Lesson Three

Large windowpanes, windows next to doors, sliding glass doors and other doors with glass, shower doors, and mirrors are all subject to human impact and pose a potential safety hazard if broken. In general, the Uniform Building Code requires all glass elements of a house located within 18 inches of the floor to be of safety glass (tempered glass). The words "safety glass" or "tempered glass" with a monogram are etched on all panes of safety glass.

SMOKE ALARMS

In many states, new homes are required to have permanently built-in smoke alarms. Many jurisdictions require smoke alarm installations in buildings that are being sold. Smoke alarms save hundreds of lives each year, and we advise that every residence have such alarms in appropriate locations. Brokers and agents should document the existence or absence of smoke alarms.

OTHER SAFETY HAZARDS

Brokers and agents should be alert for additional safety hazards, that may not be covered herein.

Lesson Three

LESSON THREE QUIZ

Answer the following questions based on the material contained in Lesson Three.

1. When inspecting a basement or crawl space for Red Flags, you should always ask the owner questions concerning

    A. visible cracks in the slab.
    B. water accumulation or abnormal moisture conditions.
    C. ceiling height.
    D. expansion possibilities.

2. Cracks develop in the walls of houses for a number of reasons. The most common reason for cracks in walls is

    A. differential movement of the structure.
    B. foundation movement.
    C. drying and shrinkage in the wooded framing members of the house.
    D. blasting from a rock quarry.

3. It not uncommon for a home owner to patch and paint prior to putting the home on the market. In doing so they often inadvertently conceal indications of Red Flags. All of the following are common types of Red Flags that may be concealed EXCEPT

    A. wall cracks.
    B. wall stains.
    C. sagging floors.
    D. sticking doors.

4. In a typical home floors are sufficiently level. There are two simple test that revel the levelness of a floor. One is the "Shuffle Walk Test," the other is

    A. the "Ball-Rolling Test."
    B. the "Rolling-Pin Test."
    C. the "Line-of-Sight Test."
    D. the "Plumb-Bob Test."

5. Movement of walls and floors can affect the operating ability of doors and windows. There are two Red Flags that detect this movement in doors and windows, one is sticking when opened or closed, the other is

    A. when cracking appears on the door or window.
    B. the mitered joints in the window or door trim separate.
    C. when the door or window will not lock.
    D. uneven spaces between windows or doors and their frames.

Lesson Three

6. When inspecting a home that has a fireplace, a few hairline cracks may be seen where the edge of the fireplace meets the wall. These are usually not serious and are not Red Flags because

   A. they occur for no reason.
   B. they occur around all fireplaces.
   C. they occur because most fireplace structures, on a pounds-per-square-foot-basis, are much lighter than the house structure and the home may settle, even if the fireplace doesn't.
   D. they occur because most fireplace structures, on a pounds-per-square-foot-basis, are much heavier than the house structure and may settle, even if the home doesn't.

7. How many major mechanical systems are contained in the average home?

   A. 2   B. 4
   C. 6   D. 8

8. A major development, in one of the mechanical systems, in a residence is a Ground Fault Interrupter (GFI). A GFI is

   A. a warning device in the event of an earthquake by indicating the severity of the shock.
   B. a cushioning device to absorb the shock waves in the event of an earthquake.
   C. a device that automatically shuts off the water supply in the event off an earthquake.
   D. a special electrical outlet (plug-in unit) that acts as a circuit breaker to shut off the electric current so fast that a hazardous current never develops.

9. All water heaters should be equipped with

   A. Ground Fault Interrupters.
   B. a method of properly venting carbon monoxide gas.
   C. a temperature/pressure relief valve.
   D. double heating elements.

10. A Red Flag condition on an electric water heater, in a garage, is indicated when

    A. it is not mounted on a platform at least eighteen (18) inches above the garage floor.
    B. it is not properly provided with combustion air.
    C. shows signs of rust and water spots at and around the base.
    D. it is not at least 24 inches from the nearest combustible wall material.

LESSON FOUR

RED FLAGS ASSOCIATED WITH ENVIRONMENTAL HAZARDS AND HAZARDOUS MATERIALS

LEARNING OBJECTIVES

Upon completion of Lesson Four you will:

1. Be aware of the adverse effects of hazardous materials on residential property values.

2. Learn the various types of hazardous material that may be present in a residential property.

3. Understand where hazardous materials may be located in a residential property.

4. Learn the Red Flag indicators identifying these materials and the names of various federal agencies that can provide additional information.

HAZARDOUS MATERIALS

Hazardous materials are a problem that can adversely affect property values, sometimes dramatically, although they have only recently been recognized as serious health issues. It has been just in the last few years that asbestos has been eliminated from home construction products and states have passed disclosure laws and instituted stricter storage and cleanup regulations for toxic waste.

Although it is very difficult for a non-professional inspector to detect many such hazards, there are a number of clues which could indicate the possibility of a potential environmental hazard on residential property.

Such hazards could stem from an old underground fuel or heating oil tank or an observation or knowledge that the property has been used for non-residential purposes. Observation of any of the following possibilities and any others that may strike you as "unusual" for a residential site would constitute an environmental Red Flag.

Observation of these or any other Red Flags does not mean that an environmental hazard exists, but with the increased sensitivity to the hazards and expense of environmental contamination in today's real estate market, disclosure of such is increasingly important.

Lesson Four

In the event that there is any concern, an environmental hazard inspection by an appropriate expert is prudent.

ASBESTOS

The following information concerning asbestos has been adapted from materials prepared by the U.S. Consumer Product Safety Commission (CPSC) and the U.S. Environmental Protection Agency (EPA) for distribution to consumers. Copies of this material in booklet form titled "Asbestos in the Home" are available from the EPA for use by interested homeowners and prospective purchasers.

Asbestos is a mineral fiber found in rocks. There are several kinds of asbestos fibers, all of which are fire-resistant and not easily destroyed or degraded by natural processes.

Asbestos has been shown to cause cancer of the lung and stomach according to studies of workers and others exposed to asbestos. There is no level of exposure to asbestos fibers that experts can assure is completely safe.

Some asbestos materials can break into small fibers which can float in the air, and these fibers can be inhaled. You cannot see these tiny fibers, and they are so small that they pass through the filters of normal vacuum cleaners and return to the air. Once inhaled, asbestos fibers can become lodged in tissue for a long time. After many years, cancer or mesothelioma can develop.

In order to be a health risk, asbestos fibers must be released from the material and be present in the air for people to breathe.

Not all asbestos products pose a health risk. A health risk exists only when asbestos fibers are released from the material or product. Soft, easily crumbled asbestos-containing material has the greatest potential for asbestos release and therefore has the greatest potential to create health risks.

Most people exposed to small amounts of asbestos do not develop any related health problems. Health studies of asbestos workers and others, however, show that the chances of developing some serious illnesses, including lung cancer, are greater after exposure to asbestos.

Asbestos has been used in a wide variety of products, including household and building materials, such as appliances, ceilings, wall and pipe coverings, floor tiles, and some roofing materials.

Basically, asbestos has been used in products for four reasons: 1) to strengthen the product material; 2) for thermal insulation within a product; 3) for thermal or acoustical insulation or decoration on exposed surfaces; and 4) for fire protection.

Lesson Four

The manufacturer of a product may be able to tell you, based on the model number and age of the product, whether or not the product contains asbestos. People who have frequently worked with asbestos (such as plumbers, building contractors, or heating contractors) often are able to make a reasonable judgment, based on a visual inspection whether or not a material contains asbestos.

When checking for Red Flags, take care to look for the following indications that a buyer may wish to seek professional advice about the existence of asbestos and its removal.

Vinyl Floor Tiles and Vinyl Sheet Flooring Asbestos has been added to some vinyl floor tiles to strengthen them. Asbestos is also present in the backing on some vinyl sheet flooring. The asbestos is often bound in the tiles and backing with vinyl or some type of binder. Asbestos fibers can be released if the tiles are sanded or seriously damaged, or if the backing on the sheet flooring is dry-scraped or sanded.

Patching Compounds and Textured Paint In 1977, CPSC banned asbestos-containing patching compounds. Some wall and ceiling joints may be patched with asbestos-containing material manufactured before 1977. If the material is in good condition, it is best to leave it alone. Sanding and scraping will release asbestos fibers.

Some textured paint sold before 1978 contained asbestos. It is unlikely that asbestos is being added to textured paint today, based on information obtained from manufacturers by the CPSC. As with patching compounds, textured paint is best left alone if undamaged. Sanding or cutting a surface with textured paint that may contain asbestos should be avoided.

Ceilings Some large buildings and a few homes built or remodeled between 1945 and 1978 may contain a crumbly, asbestos containing material which has been either sprayed or troweled onto the ceiling or walls. If the material is in good condition, it is best to leave it alone. If the material appears damaged, the owner or buyer may want to consider having it repaired or removed.

If possible, contact the builder or the contractor who applied the ceiling coating to determine whether asbestos-containing material was used.

STOVES AND FURNACES

Stove Insulation Asbestos-containing cement sheets, millboard and paper have been used frequently in homes where wood-burning stoves have been installed. These materials are used as thermal insulation to protect the floor and walls around the stoves. The cement sheet labels should tell you if the sheet contains asbestos.

Lesson Four

The cement sheet material probably will not release asbestos fibers unless scraped. This sheet material may be coated with a high temperature paint, which will help seal any asbestos into the material.

Asbestos paper or millboard is also used as a type of thermal insulation. If these materials have been placed where they are subjected to wear, there is an increased possibility that asbestos fibers may be released. Damage or misuse of the insulating material by sanding, drilling, or sawing will also release asbestos fibers.

Furnace Insulation Oil, coal, or wood furnaces with asbestos-containing insulation and cement are generally found in older homes. Updating the system to oil or gas can result in removal or damage to the old insulation. If the insulation on or around the furnace is in good condition, it is best to leave it alone. If it's in poor condition, or pieces are breaking off, the owner or buyer may want to consider having it repaired or removed.

Door Gaskets Some door gaskets in furnaces, ovens, and wood and coal stoves may contain asbestos. The asbestos-containing door gaskets on wood and coal-burning stoves are subject to wear and can release asbestos fibers under normal use conditions.

WALLS AND PIPES

Pipe Insulation Hot water and steam pipes in some older homes may be covered with an asbestos-containing material primarily to reduce heat loss, and to protect nearby surfaces from the hot pipes. Pipes may be wrapped in an asbestos "blanket" or asbestos paper tape, asbestos-containing insulation has also been used on furnace ducts. Most asbestos pipe insulation in homes was pre-formed to fit around various diameter pipes. This type of asbestos-containing insulation was manufactured from 1920 to 1972.

Wall and Ceiling Insulation Homes constructed between 1930 and 1950 may contain insulation made with asbestos. Wall and ceiling insulation that contains asbestos is generally found inside the wall or ceiling ("sandwiched" behind plaster walls). Renovation and home improvements may expose and disturb the materials.

APPLIANCES

Some appliances are, or have been, manufactured with asbestos-containing parts or components. The CPSC is making an effort to identify household appliances which could release asbestos fibers during use. The CPSC has reviewed information on the use of asbestos-containing parts in broilers, dishwashers, refrigerators, ovens, ranges, and clothes dryers.

Lesson Four

There has been a general decline in the use of asbestos in these appliances during recent years. When asbestos is used, it is in parts which will probably not result in the release of asbestos fibers during use. It is unlikely that asbestos components in these appliances present a significant health risk from release of asbestos fibers.

ROOFING SHINGLES, AND SIDING

Some roofing shingles, siding shingles and sheets have been manufactured with asbestos-using portland cement as a binding agent. Since these products are already in place and outdoors, there is likely to be little risk to human health. However, if the siding is worn or damaged, the owner or buyer may spraypaint it to help seal in the fibers.

HOW TO IDENTIFY ASBESTOS

You should first try to determine whether the material does in fact contain asbestos. Avoid disturbing the material if at all possible. If you cannot determine from the label, installer, or manufacturer whether the material contains asbestos, it is best to assume that the product contains asbestos.

People who have frequently worked with asbestos material (such as plumbers, building contractors or heating contractors) often are able to make a reasonable judgment about whether or not a product contains asbestos, based on a visual inspection. If you are uncertain whether some materials contain asbestos, you may want to call such people for advice.

TOXIC WASTE

There was a time when waste disposal problems--water wells polluted by septic systems, or streams polluted by sewage outfalls --were regarded as isolated events no one could do much about until after a leak was detected.

Some wastes can be highly toxic and long-lived, and toxic substances can pollute water supplies that serve an entire community, pollute the ground a community is built on, or even contaminate food if it is grown on polluted soils or irrigated with polluted water.

Water quality has become a significant public safety issue. Water well pollution from industrial sources, soil pollution in toxic dumps near or over which housing developments have been constructed (as in Love Canal, New York), and contamination of communities by floods carrying toxic runoff (as in Times Beach, Florida), continually reemphasize the need for communities to take precautions against pollution.

RADON

The following information concerning Radon has been adapted from materials prepared by the U.S. Environmental Protection Agency (EPA) for distribution to consumers. Copies of this material in booklet form, titled "A Citizen's Guide to Radon" are available from the EPA for use by interested homeowners and prospective purchasers.

Radon is a naturally occurring radioactive gas. You cannot see it, smell it, or taste it. Radon comes from the natural breakdown (radioactive decay) of uranium. Radon can be found in high concentrations in soils and rocks containing uranium, granite, shale, phosphate and pitch blende. Radon may also be found in soils contaminated with certain types of industrial wastes, such as the by-products from uranium or phosphate mining.

In outdoor air, radon is diluted to such low concentrations that it does not represent a safety hazard. However, once inside an enclosed space (such as a home) radon can accumulate. Indoor levels depend on a building's construction and the concentration of radon in the underlying soil.

The only known health effect associated with exposure to elevated levels of radon is an increased risk of developing lung cancer. Not everyone exposed to elevated levels of radon will develop lung cancer, and the time between exposure and the onset of the disease may be many years.

Radon has always been present in the air. Concern about elevated indoor concentrations first arose in the late 1960s when homes were found in the West that had been built with materials contaminated by waste from uranium mines. Since then, cases of high indoor radon levels resulting from industrial activities have been found in many parts of the country. We have only recently become aware, however, that houses in various parts of the U.S. may have high indoor radon levels caused by natural deposits of uranium in the soil on which they are built.

Most houses in this country are not likely to have a radon problem; but relatively few houses do have highly elevated levels. The dilemma is that, right now, no one knows which houses have a problem and which do not. You may wish to call your state radiation protection office to find out if any high levels have been discovered in your area.

How does Radon get into a home? Radon is a gas which can move through small spaces in the soil and rock on which a house is built. Radon can seep into a home through dirt floors, cracks in concrete floors and walls, floor drains, sumps, joints, and tiny cracks or pores in hollow-block walls.

Radon also can enter water within private wells and be released into a home when the water is used. Usually, radon is not a problem with large community water supplies, where it would likely be released into the outside air before the water reaches a home. (For more information concerning radon in water, contact your state's radiation protection office.)

In some unusual situations, radon may be released from the materials used in the construction of a home. For example, this may be a problem if a house has a large stone fireplace or has a solar heating system in which heat is stored in large beds of stone. In general, however, building materials are not a major source of indoor radon.

Since you cannot see or smell radon, special equipment is needed to detect it. The two most popular detectors are the charcoal canister and the alpha track detector. Both of these devices are exposed to the air in your home for a specified period of time and sent to a laboratory for analysis.

There are other techniques--requiring operation by trained personnel--which can be used to measure radon levels, but such techniques may be more expensive than the devices shown above.

UNDERGROUND STORAGE TANKS/HAZARDOUS WASTE

Pipes, usually 2 to 2 1/2 inches in diameter, emerging from the ground that are capped or have a 180 degree bend at the top are Red Flags. Such pipes are common as vent pipes for underground fuel and solvent tanks.

Additional Red Flags include:

- oil spots on the ground or areas that are dark brown to black where vegetation will not grow;

- holes, two or three inches in diameter, in garage floors set so that fluids can flow into them (sumps);

- evidence of extensive paint or chemical storage facilities; or

- evidence of facilities or equipment indicating mechanical or fabrication work at that location.

Question the seller on past uses of the property. Was there a photographer who emptied photographic chemicals out back? Did someone run a "home" car repair or furniture refinishing business?

Lesson Four

Although it is not part of a "visual" inspection of the home, it's prudent to review title documents to see if the property is listed as having been used for something other than a residence.

Evidence of these Red Flags suggests that the prudent agent ask whether there is an underground tank on the property. If there is, many states have regulations requiring the tanks removal if they haven't been used in 6 months or some similar time period. Evidence of underground tanks can also trigger investigation into possible contamination. This can lead to *very* expensive problems potentially. Whoever owns property *today* must pay for the clean-up --even if they weren't responsible for the contamination.

LEAD HAZARDS FROM PIPES AND PAINT

What is lead poisoning? Lead poisoning occurs when the body contains a high concentration of lead. The effects of lead poisoning can cause paralysis, brain damage, and convulsions.

Lead is regulated by the Environmental Protection Agency through its authority in the Resource Conservation and Recovery Act (RCRA). The presence of lead in the water we drink or the paint used in a home is very dangerous. Children tend to absorb more lead than adults and they are more likely to exhibit hand-to-mouth behavior.

Drinking water Drinking water can become contaminated as it passes through lead pipes. In the late 1930s lead water pipes were still being used. In 1986 the Safe Drinking Water Act required the use of "lead-free" solder, pipes and flux for facilities connected to public water systems. Congress, in 1988, banned the use of lead-based solder in plumbing applications in homes and buildings.

Lead-based paint The most probable places where lead-based paint will be found in a home are in the bathroom and kitchen walls, woodwork and window frames. The use of lead paint was prohibited in 1980.

Although a visual inspection can not determine whether a hazard exists, there are Red Flags that may indicate a thorough investigation is warranted. Checking for the presence of lead-based paint requires removing a sample and having it tested by a qualified laboratory.

The probability of lead-based paint having been used in a structure is directly related to its age. Studies have shown that lead-based paint was used in two thirds of homes built prior to 1940 and one third of homes built from 1940 to 1960. A smaller percentage of houses built between 1960 and 1980 were found to contain lead-based paint. You should be aware that commercial facilities in which metal work, automobile radiator repairs, and soldering activities

Lesson Four

were carried out are also very likely places for lead contamination.

HUD warns that three out of four homes built prior to 1978 have lead-based paint.

A Red Flag is related to the age of the home. Any home built before 1980 may contain lead-based paint. A rule of thumb would be, "The older the home the greater the possibility of lead-based paint."

Lesson Four

LESSON FOUR QUIZ

Answer the following questions based on the material contained in Lesson Four.

1. In order to be a health risk, asbestos fibers

    A. must be released from the material and be present in the air for people to breathe.
    B. must be released from the material and be ingested with liquid.
    C. must be released from the material and come in contact with the skin.
    D. must be released from the material and subjected to ultraviolet light.

2. Asbestos has been used in products for four basic reasons. Which of the following is NOT one of the basic reason for using asbestos?

    A. To strengthen the product material
    B. For decoration on exposed surfaces
    C. For fire protection
    D. For its color enhancing properties

3. In your inspection of an older home you discover a decorative textured ceiling, which is in good shape, but which you suspect contains asbestos. You should

    A. recommend that the homeowner scrape the texture off the ceiling before painting.
    B. recommend that the homeowner leave the texture alone.
    C. not mention you suspect the presence of asbestos.
    D. recommend that the homeowner paint the ceiling to hide the texture.

4. In older homes materials containing asbestos may be found

    A. in wood-burning stove insulation.
    B. in furnace insulation.
    C. in door gaskets in furnaces and wood stoves.
    D. All of the above

5. When making improvements or renovations on homes built between 1930 and 1950 the exposing and disturbance of asbestos is not an important consideration.

    A. True
    B. False

Lesson Four 54

6. Some roofing shingles and siding shingles have been manufactured with asbestos, using portland cement as a binding agent. These products when present and in good condition, on an older home, are likely to be of little risk to human health.

    A. True
    B. False

7. Radon gas comes from the natural breakdown of uranium. Radon gas has always been present in the air, however, radon gas is a health hazard only when found in high concentrations. Such concentrations are usually found

    A. outside of a home.
    B. inside a home.
    C. near the outside walls of a home.
    D. in the airspace immediately above a home.

8. Underground storage tanks can be containers for possible hazardous waste material. All of the following are Red Flags EXCEPT

    A. dark brown spots on the ground where vegetation will not grow.
    B. a hole, two or three inches in diameter, in garage floors set so that fluids can flow into them.
    C. pipes, usually 2 to 2 1/2 inches in diameter, emerging from the ground that are capped or have a 180 degree bend at the top.
    D. abundantly producing vegetable garden.

9. Evidence of underground tanks can trigger investigation into possible contamination. This can lead to potentially very expensive problems. If contamination is found to exist, who pays for the clean-up?

    A. The previous owner
    B. The owner who is responsible for the contamination
    C. The present owner
    D. All owners share equally.

10. If while conducting a listing inspection of a home you have any suspicions of the presence of hazardous waste material, the prudent action is to

    A. turn down the listing to avoid exposure to risk.
    B. say nothing to the home owner.
    C. reveal your suspicions to the owner.
    D. reveal your suspicions and ask the owners of their knowledge of the past uses of the property.